"William I. Robinson elucidates the terrifying configurations of a new type of global dictatorship, that imposed by transnational capital. By seizing control of national economies and imposing the most sophisticated forms of surveillance in human history these transnational entities are cementing into place a dystopian world that serves the interests of a global elite at the expense of liberty, freedom of expression, democracy, and economic security. This is the future, unless we rise up to wrest power back from our corporate overlords."
—Chris Hedges, author of *America, the Farewell Tour*

"As an axis of rampant capital and wondrous technology grows by the day and liberal democracy sheds its last illusions, William I. Robinson describes a true enemy of humanity that is close to home. And yet nothing is inevitable. Read this urgent book."
—John Pilger, journalist, writer, and documentary filmmaker

"A novel and important analysis of how global capitalism is being transformed by the pandemic. Robinson skillfully maps out how expanding digitalization, growing government intervention, and emerging movements across the political spectrum all reflect and reshape ongoing capitalist crises."
—Nick Srnicek, program director, MSc Digital Economy, King's College London, and author of *Platform Capitalism*

T0007464

"Globalization's first episode in the history of our species was the out-migration of Homo sapiens from Africa to the rest of the planet. Today's globalization builds on the out-migration that resulted in colonialism and neocolonialism, imperialism, and neoliberalism. Those who once cheered the colonialist onslaught are now reeling from what neoliberalism is bringing to their bodies: literally a war for survival that takes place in their own bloodstreams. Thus, the rapacious greed that put a banker between a student and a professor wants to turn health professionals into 'agents of repression.' From the 2001 Dark Winter bio-terror war game to the 2010 Lockstep report that presaged today's coronavirus pandemic, to 2019's Event 201, to 2021's Cyber Polygon, agents of global capital have been unequivocal about what is in store for us. The true question is: 'What are we prepared to do to stop them?' Professor Robinson is clear that there are many possible futures. Readers of this book will also understand that they have the power to reject reformist 'revolutions from the top' that include 'Inclusive Capitalism' within a global police state. Now is the time for the people to organically reject the 'offers' of the global capitalist class and make real the revolution of our values; that is, one of truth, justice, peace, and human and earth dignity."

—Cynthia McKinney, author, activist, six-term member of the United States Congress

Praise for *Global Police State* (2020)

"Karl Marx aspired to a world in which our animal needs would be satisfied and our human needs could be addressed. It is a realistic possibility now, as William I. Robinson outlines—or the alternative that is taking shape before our eyes: a "global police state" controlled by narrowly concentrated capital, with "surplus humanity" left to survive somehow on its own. The choice is in our hands. There could hardly be a more compelling one."
—Noam Chomsky, Institute professor emeritus, Massachusetts Institute of Technology (MIT), author of *Who Rules the World?*

"For the last twenty years, William I. Robinson has been one of the most important analysts of global capitalism and the dynamics of globalization. In this new work, Robinson turns his attention to the emergence of a twenty-first century 'global police state' that has developed as a corollary to growing inequality, climate collapse, and intensifying migration movements of the dispossessed. As Robinson warns, with great deprivation comes great repression, policing, and potentially war. Robinson writes pointedly and with urgency for a broad audience with an interest in mobilizing for a just world."
—Keeanga-Yamahtta Taylor, professor of African American Studies, Princeton University, author of *From #BlackLives Matter to Black Liberation*

Praise for *Into the Tempest* (2018)

"This book is a treasury of big-picture insights from our leading theorist of the emerging system of global capitalism. William I. Robinson's project—to understand the political economy in order to change it—stands as the preeminent successor to Marx's project from an earlier epoch. For readers perplexed about our changing world and apprehensive about its future, here is your primer and call to action."

—Paul Raskin, founding president of the Tellus Institute, author of *Journey to Earthland*

"William I. Robinson offers those engaged in the struggle against global capitalism a remarkable and compelling insight and framework in order to both understand our opponents and to better grasp the strengths and weaknesses of the oppressed and dispossessed. This is the book for which I have been waiting, and I could not put it down."

—Bill Fletcher, Jr., trade unionist, author of *They're Bankrupting Us: And Twenty Other Myths About Unions*

GLOBAL CIVIL WAR

KAIROS

In ancient Greek philosophy, *kairos* signifies the right time or the "moment of transition." We believe that we live in such a transitional period. The most important task of social science in time of transformation is to transform itself into a force of liberation. Kairos, an editorial imprint of the Anthropology and Social Change department housed in the California Institute of Integral Studies, publishes groundbreaking works in critical social sciences, including anthropology, sociology, geography, theory of education, political ecology, political theory, and history.

Series editor: Andrej Grubačić

Recent and featured Kairos books:

Taming the Rascal Multitude: Essays, Interviews, and Lectures 1997–2014 by Noam Chomsky

A New World in Our Hearts: Noam Chomsky in Conversation with Michael Albert

Between Thought and Expression Lies a Lifetime: Why Ideas Matter by Noam Chomsky and James Kelman

Mutual Aid: An Illuminated Factor of Evolution by Peter Kropotkin, illustrated by N.O. Bonzo

Asylum for Sale: Profit and Protest in the Migration Industry edited by Siobhán McGuirk and Adrienne Pine

Building Free Life: Dialogues with Öcalan edited by International Initiative

The Art of Freedom: A Brief History of the Kurdish Liberation Struggle by Havin Guneser

The Sociology of Freedom: Manifesto of the Democratic Civilization, Volume III by Abdullah Öcalan

Facebooking the Anthropocene in Raja Ampat by Bob Ostertag

In, Against, and Beyond Capitalism: The San Francisco Lectures by John Holloway

For more information visit www.pmpress.org/blog/kairos/

GLOBAL CIVIL WAR

CAPITALISM POST-PANDEMIC

William I. Robinson

KAIROS

Global Civil War: Capitalism Post-Pandemic
William I. Robinson © 2022
This edition © PM Press

ISBN: 978–1–62963–938–3 (paperback)
ISBN: 978–1–62963–953–6 (ebook)
Library of Congress Control Number: 2021945055

Cover design by John Yates/www.stealworks.com
Interior design by briandesign

10 9 8 7 6 5 4 3 2 1

PM Press
PO Box 23912
Oakland, CA 94623
www.pmpress.org

Printed in the USA

CONTENTS

ACKNOWLEDGMENTS

The list of people I am in indebted to for my own intellectual and political development is vast. Moreover, intellectual production is always a collective product of social labor. All I can do here is thank the handful of people who provided direct assistance and encouragement with regard to the research and preparation of this study. My research assistant Lingxiao Chen prepared most of the tables that appear in the book. My wife Venus Leung read over the entire manuscript and provided critical feedback. Salvador Rangel read chapters one and two and provided indispensable comments and suggestions. Thanks also to Rosemary Lee, Cynthia McKinney, Steven Miller, Jason Moore, Hoai-An Nguyen, Oscar Soto, Nick Srnicek, Manfred Steger, and Kees van der Pijl. Throughout 2020 and 2021, I was in close and fruitful correspondence with Neil Faulkner and Phil Hearst as we attempted to analyze the global crisis as it has played out and to identify the most urgent tasks of radical intellectuals and the left. I am grateful to them and to the UK-based Anti-Capitalist Resistance organization with which they are involved. A special thanks to Ramsey Kanaan, Andrej Grubačić, Jonathan Rowland, and Michael Ryan at PM Press. Apologies to anyone I may have inadvertently left out. Needless to say, I alone am responsible for the manuscript, including all errors, omissions, and deficiencies.

LIST OF ACRONYMS

3D	three-dimensional
5G	Fifth Generation Broadband
AI	artificial intelligence
BLM	Black Lives Matter
GB	Gigabyte
GDP	Gross Domestic Product
CEO	chief executive officer
CIT	Computer and Information Technology
EU	European Union
GOF	gain of function
IoT	Internet of Things
IP	Internet Protocol
ILO	International Labour Organization
IMF	International Monetary Fund
MAS	Movement Toward Socialism
OWS	Occupy Wall Street
PPE	Personal Protective Equipment
TCC	Transnational Capitalist Class
TNS	Transnational State
S&P	Standard and Poors
WHO	World Health Organization
WSF	World Social Forum
UNCTAD	United Nations Conference on Trade and Development
US	United States

GLOBAL CAPITALISM POST-PANDEMIC

Not far from my home in Los Angeles are about a hundred houses that have been boarded up for years. The houses were bought by the city in the late twentieth century through eminent domain to make way for an extension of the 710 freeway that dead ends in my El Sereno neighborhood. But opposition from affluent communities further east eventually killed the project, leaving the houses to lie vacant. Meanwhile, on any given night in 2020, there were some 130,000 homeless people in the city, a thousand of whom died in the streets in the first ten months of that year. One may imagine that this homeless crisis was the result of a shortage of housing. Yet, in 2020, there was a surplus of luxury homes, so much so that 93,000 housing units in the city lay vacant. The problem was not the lack of housing units but the lack of profits to be made by the corporate real estate developers who could not find enough high-income people to rent or purchase their speculative investment properties. In fact, nearly 70 percent of residential units in the city were owned by these corporate developers and investment funds, which also owned 76 percent of all empty lots, accounting for twenty-two square miles of vacant land.[1]

As the coronavirus ripped through Los Angeles, and as many families who lost employment due to pandemic closures faced eviction from their rental units, homeless and housing rights activists stepped up their struggle for shelter, fearful that the virus placed those living in the streets at great risk. Organized into a "Reclaim and Rebuild Our Community" movement, twenty unhoused families who were living in cars and encampments, with the support of several hundred peaceful community activists, removed the boarding in a number of the empty state-owned houses one cold winter day on the eve of the 2020 Thanksgiving holiday and settled in. But the comfort of a roof over their head did not last long. At least fifty police patrol vehicles surrounded the homes on the very night before the holiday to violently evict the occupants, for the most part mothers and young children. The police used battering rams to knock down doors, hog-tying and dragging out anyone who resisted and arresting sixty-two people for trespassing and burglary.[2]

The violence and cruelty of city authorities against its most vulnerable residents is emblematic of what took place around the world in the face of the Covid-19 contagion. If humanity survives into the twenty-second century, historians will surely look back at the pandemic as a before-and-after turning point. In a period of weeks, the global economy tumbled into freefall, with losses estimated at over $8 trillion in just the first six months of the contagion. The pandemic was devastating for the world's poor majority, as hundreds of millions faced unemployment, poverty, hunger, and death. Contrary to popular perception, the pandemic did not cause the crisis of global capitalism, for this was already upon us. It did, however, intensify this crisis many times over, further catalyzing trends and processes well underway prior to the outbreak. If the pandemic was a time of great suffering and deprivation for several billion people, it was also a golden opportunity for ruling classes to increase their wealth and to heighten their control and surveillance. It set off political and civil strife around the world, as governments, unable to cope with the fallout, were exposed as callous instruments of wealth and corruption. The health emergency will have already passed by the time many readers turn these pages, but the crisis of global capitalism will be with us into the foreseeable future.

The pandemic is, therefore, but a staging point for a larger story. This book is about the world that is emerging in the wake of the plague. The extent of polarization of wealth and power, of deprivation and misery, among the world's poor majority, already defied belief prior to the outbreak. In 2018, just seventeen global financial conglomerates collectively managed $41.1 trillion dollars, more than half the GDP of the entire planet. That same year, the richest 1 percent of humanity led by 36 million millionaires and 2,400 billionaires controlled more than half of the world's wealth, while the bottom 80 percent—nearly six billion people—had to make do with just 5 percent of this wealth. The result is devastation for the majority. Worldwide, 50 percent of all people live on less than $2.50 a day and a full 80 percent live on less than $10 per day. One in three people on the planet suffers from some form of malnutrition, nearly a billion go to bed hungry each night, and another two billion suffer from food insecurity. Refugees from war, climate change, political repression, and economic collapse already number into the hundreds of millions.

Such savage inequalities are explosive. They fuel mass protest by the oppressed and lead the ruling groups to deploy an ever more omnipresent global police state to contain the rebellion of the global working and popular classes. Global capitalism is emerging from the pandemic in a dangerous new phase. The contradictions of this crisis-ridden system have reached the breaking point, placing the world in a perilous situation that borders on global civil war. The stakes could not be higher. The battle for the post-pandemic world is now being waged. This book provides the "big picture" synthesis of a global capitalism mired in deep crisis, cascading social and political conflict, and the breakdown of the post–World War II international order. My hope is that this "big picture" will help readers contextualize the current worldwide political conjuncture as we tumble toward global civil war and step into an unknown future.

THE DIGITALIZED DICTATORSHIP

The centerpiece of the book is a novel analysis of the radical restructuring of transformation of global capitalism based on a much more advanced digitalization of the entire global economy and society and of the social and political struggles breaking out worldwide around this process. I have been researching and writing about capitalist globalization for three decades. The system was in the midst of this novel wave of transformation when the outbreak hit, turbocharging the process and rousing new waves of popular struggle. In my earlier works, I identified globalization as a new epoch in the ongoing and open-ended evolution of world capitalism, characterized by the rise of truly transnational capital and the integration of every country into a new globalized system of production, finance, and services. I have aspired over the years to carry out such theoretical work, because this transformation of world capitalism starting in the late twentieth century forms the backdrop to the burning political matters of our day.

We must remember that collective agency constantly shapes and reshapes structures, which themselves are momentary historical ossifications of such agency, so that all social theory is historical and must keep pace with the dynamics of change. Twenty-first century capitalism is very different from earlier variants of the system that developed in previous centuries. I began to research world capitalism in the 1980s, on the heels of the late twentieth-century worldwide defeat and reversal of the left's fortunes, of the world's first experiments—however flawed—in socialism, and of the Third World national liberation struggles. In the 1990s, I sought explanations for the end of this cycle and for the rise of neoliberalism in the profound transformations of the world political economy and the global system. Through a series of concrete historical investigations over these years, my ideas developed into a theory of global capitalism, which I initially laid out in a 2004 study, *A Theory of Global Capitalism*. In 2008, when world capitalism lurched into its most severe recession since the 1930s depression—what some refer to as the Great Recession—I turned my attention more fully to the topic of global crisis, publishing *Global Capitalism and the Crisis of Humanity* in 2014.

As the crisis deepened in the past few years, I came to focus on the increasingly repressive, even totalitarian, nature of the system, captured in my 2020 book *The Global Police State*.[3] The study before you builds on my previous research and takes it in new directions. My objective was to write a succinct book intended as a hybrid between an academic study and an essay spanning three relatively short chapters and the briefest of conclusions that, far from exhausting the discussion, points readers to what is coming in the years ahead. Radical political economy is a revolutionary tool, but it can sometimes be daunting. While I have strived to make this work accessible, there are a few passages at the start of chapter one that must be tackled by those not familiar with some core concepts of radical political economy, which I attempt to walk the reader through. Otherwise, I hope that I have provided an eminently readable study that lays out in broad strokes the post-pandemic world of global capitalism we are entering, wracked by conflict, contradiction, suffering, and struggle.

Chapter one, "A General Crisis of Capitalist Rule," starts with an overview of the crisis of global capitalism. It is both an economic, or structural, crisis of stagnation and a political crisis of state legitimacy and capitalist hegemony. It is also existential because of the threat of ecological collapse, as well as the renewed threat of nuclear war, to which we must add the danger of future pandemics that may involve much deadlier microbes than coronaviruses. The pandemic lockdowns served as dry runs for how digitalization may allow the dominant groups to step up restructuring time and space and to exercise greater control over the global working class. The system is now pushing toward expansion through militarization, wars, and conflicts, through a new round of violent dispossession, and through further plunder of the state. Historically, epidemics dramatically alter the political, social, and economic landscape. Throughout history they have been a force for upheaval and often radical change in society. The black death that ravaged Europe from 1347 to 1352 killed an estimated twenty-five to thirty million people, anywhere between 30 and 60 percent of the entire European population. The plague severely reduced the labor supply for European feudalism, raised the price of labor, and strengthened serfs in their struggles against landlords and aristocracies. In this way, the aftermath of the plague threw European feudalism into a terminal crisis and eventually generated conditions propitious for the rise of capitalism. The Covid-19 pandemic is similarly altering the global landscape.

Chapter two, "Digitalization and the Transformation of Global Capitalism," analyzes a new round of restructuring and transformation based on a much more advanced digitalization of the entire global economy and society; on the application of so-called fourth industrial revolution technologies. Here I build on and branch away from other studies on digitalization, of which there have been many in recent years, applying my global capitalism theory to this process and focusing especially on changes in capitalist social and class relations. The changing social and economic conditions brought about by the pandemic and its aftermath are accelerating the process. These conditions have helped a new bloc of transnational capital, led by the giant tech companies, interwoven as it is with finance, pharmaceuticals, and the military-industrial complex, to amass ever greater power and to consolidate control over the commanding heights of the global economy. As restructuring proceeds, it heightens the concentration of capital worldwide, worsens social inequality, and aggravates international tensions. Enabled by digital applications, the ruling groups are turning to ratcheting up the global police state to contain social upheavals. What the reader will find in this chapter is not a blueprint, much less an exhaustive account of the new wave of capitalist transformation, but an approximation, by which I mean an attempt to identify emerging trends and configurations so as to advance an outline of what we may expect as we peer into the future.

Chapter three, "Whither the Global Revolt," surveys the proliferation of conflicts arising from the ravages of global capitalism and explores alternative futures. Capitalist crises are times of intense social and class struggles. There has been a rapid political polarization in global society since 2008 between an insurgent far right and an insurgent left. The ongoing crisis has incited popular revolts. Workers, farmers, and poor people have engaged in a wave of strikes and protests around the world. From the Sudan to Chile, France to Thailand, South Africa to the United States, a "people's spring" is breaking out everywhere. This chapter reviews the global revolt and then goes on to discuss some of the quandaries and challenges to advancing an emancipatory project. But the crisis also animates far-right and neofascist forces that have surged in many countries around the world and sought to capitalize politically on the health calamity and its aftermath. Neofascist movements and authoritarian and dictatorial regimes have proliferated around the world as democracy breaks down. Chapter three may be the most urgent for readers insofar as we strategize about how to combat the rise of neofascism, but the two chapters that precede it lay the indispensable groundwork for this strategizing.

While we typically associate dictatorship with strongmen and military rule—and, sadly, these types of dictatorship are spreading—it is clear that the world's people live under a new type of dictatorship, that of transnational capital. In recent decades transnational capital has subordinated virtually the entire world's population to its logic and domination. I mean *dictatorship* in the literal sense of the word, such that transnational capital *dictates* as it becomes more powerful, omnipresent, and deadly than any other dictatorship in history. The concentration of economic power in the hands of transnational capital generates a concentration of political power that underscores the dictatorial reach of what I call the transnational capitalist class.

The global civil war is about a struggle of humanity against this dictatorship. Simply put, the vast majority will be unable to survive for much longer should global capitalism continue down its current path. Digital transformation *may* enhance many times over the power of transnational capital to further dictate the terms of social and economic life. I italicize *may* because the intractable crisis of global capitalism generates social strife and political conflict and throws up resistance that may push back against this power. As we peer into the future, we must remind ourselves that it is not predetermined, that our collective action and contingency in historic outcomes means there are many possible futures. This dystopic digitalized dictatorship is only one possible future, albeit one that is rapidly coming into focus at this time. Thus, this book is as much a political warning as it is an analytical and a theoretical contribution to understanding contemporary global society.

Los Angeles
February 2021

CHAPTER ONE

THE CRISIS OF CAPITALIST RULE

> Covid-19 is not just a temporary crisis. [It is] a permanent disruptor. Historic global crises like wars, revolutions, pandemics, etc. often feel like they put history on fast-forward. Processes that normally take decades or longer to play out unfold in a couple of weeks. Coronavirus is the political, economic, and psychological event of our lifetimes that will drive disruption and transformation for years to come. It will bring a radical transformation of the kind that occurs only once in a generation.
>
> —Bank of America, internal report, May 2020[1]

The Covid-19 virus that spread around the world in 2020 triggered an economic meltdown and social catastrophe unmatched since the Great Depression of the 1930s. Millions of people became unemployed overnight, went hungry, lost their homes, fell ill, and faced harsh state repression. The extent of the meltdown was simply staggering. More than 90 percent of the world's countries fell into deep recession in 2020, compared to only 60 percent in the 2008 Great Recession, making it a truly *global* crisis.[2] "Beyond the staggering economic impacts, the pandemic will also have severe and long-lasting socio-economic impacts that may well weaken long-term growth prospects" warned the World Bank several months into the pandemic. There would be no quick recovery, it cautioned, given "the plunge in investment because of elevated uncertainty, the erosion of human capital from the legions of unemployed, and the potential for ruptures of trade and supply linkages."[3] Economies did bounce back from the depths of the implosion, yet it was clear that economic turbulence and political conflict around the world would only escalate as the world emerged from the pandemic.

The contagion was but the spark that ignited the combustibles of a global economy that never fully recovered from the 2008 financial collapse and had been teetering on the brink of renewed crisis ever since. The political agents of global capitalism in states and the corporate media were quick to blame the meltdown on the virus, as stock markets and international commerce went into free fall. The pundits had deluded themselves into believing that all was well, but the underlying structural causes of the 2008 debacle, far from being resolved, had been steadily aggravated. On the eve of the pandemic, growth in the EU countries had already shrunk to zero, much of Latin America and sub-Saharan Africa was in recession, growth rates in Asia were steadily declining, and North America faced a slowdown. The writing was on the wall. With or without Covid-19, as we will see, the world economy has been mired in a structural crisis that is too entrenched to be considered a mere recession or even a depression.

The crisis of global capitalism, however, is more than just economic, or structural. It is also political, one of state legitimacy, even capitalist hegemony. Millions, perhaps billions, of people around the world are questioning a system they no longer see as legitimate. Some have taken a renewed interest in socialism, while others are being mobilized by far-right demagogues into neofascist projects. Capitalist states face spiraling crises of legitimacy after decades of hardship and social decay wrought by neoliberalism, aggravated by these states' inability to manage the health emergency and the economic collapse. Crises, let us recall, are times of intense social and class conflict. There has been a rapid political polarization in global society since 2008 between an insurgent far right and an insurgent left. The ongoing crisis has animated far-right and neofascist forces that have surged in many countries around the world and that sought to capitalize politically on the health calamity, but it has also roused popular struggles from below, as workers and the poor engaged in a wave of strikes and protests on every continent that shows no signs of letting up. Political systems are cracking, social orders crumbling. We have entered into a period of mounting chaos in the world capitalist system.

The global revolt has been underway for some years now and is escalating as we move into the brave new world of post-pandemic capitalism. Prior to the health emergency, the system was already headed toward what we call an *organic crisis*: a general crisis of capitalist rule. The Bolshevik leader Vladimir Lenin described the symptoms of such a situation: 1) when there is a crisis in the prevailing system, and it is impossible for the ruling classes to rule in the old way; 2) when the want and suffering of the oppressed classes have grown more acute than usual; 3) when as a consequence the masses increase their historical action. Whether or not we are headed for a revolutionary rupture with capitalism, a worldwide fascist dictatorship, or a collapse of global civilization is a matter I will discuss in chapter three. Here we can note that the health emergency, above all, served to bring into stark relief the profundity of this crisis and the extent of malaise in the global social order. The worst of the contagion eventually passed, but not before taking a heavy toll. But the crisis of global capitalism is here to stay and has become considerably more acute in the wake of the pandemic. Before I launch into a discussion of the pandemic itself we must make a brief analytical and theoretical incursion into the nature of capitalist crises. Let us start with the economic dimension.

OVERACCUMULATION AND CHRONIC STAGNATION

Despite claims to the contrary by neoclassical economists, crisis is endemic to capitalism, and instability rather than equilibrium is the natural state of the system. The history of capitalism is one of periodic crises of two types. One is cyclical, sometimes called the business cycle, and shows up as recessions. They typically occur about every ten years. There were recessions in the early 1980s, the early 1990s, and the early 2000s. The other is more serious, a structural crisis, or what I call a restructuring crisis, because its resolution requires a major restructuring of the system. Cyclical crises may affect only certain countries or regions, whereas structural crises generally affect the entire world economy. In the course of the twentieth century the system experienced two restructuring crises, the Great Depression of the 1930s and the crisis of stagnation and inflation (known as "stagflation") of the 1970s. Both these crises had their origin in what political economists call overaccumulation. This refers to a situation in which enormous amounts of capital (profits) are built up, but this capital cannot find productive outlets for reinvestment. This capital then becomes stagnant, as capitalists hold on to their accumulated profits rather than reinvesting them, throwing the system into crisis.

Overaccumulation originates in the circuit of capitalist production. In simplified terms, capitalists seek to maximize profit by constantly lowering the overall cost of labor, that is, the wage portion of the costs of production. One way to lower these costs is to lower the absolute amount paid to workers. In recent years, for instance, capitalist globalization has involved the relocation of factories and services to low-wage zones, epitomized by the spread around the world of sweatshops employing super-exploited young women. Another way is to raise productivity, that is, to raise output per worker per unit of time worked, so that fewer workers are needed for the same output. Typically, this has involved the introduction of new technologies that either replace workers entirely or that increase the productivity of each worker. Yet labor is the source of all surplus value, that is, of profits. Internal to the dynamic of capital accumulation is a tendency for the *rate* of profit to fall, even as the overall *volume* of profits may increase, because as capitalists compete with one another and strive to control labor and to reduce labor costs, they raise productivity through the ongoing introduction of new labor-saving and productivity-enhancing technologies and organizational forms. Ever less labor is required to produce ever more wealth as output per unit of labor increases. Anticipating what we will explore in the next chapter, new digital technologies that are now at the very core of the global economy have greatly increased productivity and corporate profits, even as the worldwide economic restructuring made possible by these technologies has resulted in an expanding army of the unemployed and the marginalized, or surplus humanity.

Analyzing these tendencies in the nineteenth century, Karl Marx noted that "a fall in the profit rate, and accelerated accumulation, are simply different expressions of the same process, in so far as both express the development of productivity." He continued: "In view of the fact that the rate at which the total capital is valorized, i.e. the rate of profit, is the spur to capitalist production, a fall in this rate... appears as a threat to the development of the capitalist process; it promotes overproduction, speculation and crises."[4] To reiterate, overaccumulation thus refers to how enormous amounts of capital are accumulated, yet this capital cannot be reinvested profitably and becomes stagnant, or, in Marx's words, "the capitalist would have won nothing by his own exertions but the obligation to supply more in the same labor time, in a word, more difficult conditions for the augmentation of the value of his capital."[5] In fact, while the absolute volume of transnational corporate profits has snowballed in recent years, the rate of profit has steadily declined. The average rate stood in the brief post–World War II "golden age" of world capitalism at about 15 percent. By the end of the 1980s it had dropped to 10 percent and continued to decline, to 6 percent in 2017.[6]

Although overaccumulation originates in the sphere of production, it becomes manifest in the sphere of circulation, that is, it shows up in the market as a crisis of overproduction or underconsumption. This refers to a situation in which the economy has produced—or has the capacity to produce—great quantities of wealth (defined as things that people need and want), but the market cannot absorb this wealth, because more and more people have been made surplus as technology advances and productivity increases, and/or because the wages of those that are employed are not sufficient for them to consume all that their labor produces. In other words, capitalism by its very nature will produce abundant wealth yet polarize that wealth and generate ever greater levels of social inequality. Overaccumulation appears first as a glut in the market, and then as stagnation. In fact, in the years leading up to the pandemic there was a steady rise in underutilized capacity and a slowdown in industrial production around the world.[7] The surplus of accumulated capital with nowhere to go expanded rapidly. Transnational corporations recorded record profits during the 2010s at the same time that corporate investment declined.[8] The total cash held in reserves of the world's two thousand biggest nonfinancial corporations increased from $6.6 trillion in 2010 to $14.2 trillion in 2020—considerably more than the foreign exchange reserves of the world's central governments—as the global economy stagnated.[9]

Well before the pandemic hit in 2020, all the telltale signs of an overaccumulation crisis were present. Before further analysis of this new crisis, let us return to the two early restructuring crises of the twentieth century. In the actual course of capitalist history, ongoing class and social struggles shape and constantly reshape how capitalism develops and how crises play themselves out. Mass popular and working-class struggles spread early in the twentieth century and reached a peak in the 1930s. These struggles forced capitalists into what became known as a "class compromise." Capitalists and states were forced to back down from the unrestrained free market capitalism of the nineteenth and early twentieth centuries, with its stark inequalities and deprivation of the masses. What some called the "gilded age" and the "age of the robber barons" gave way through the pressure of these mass struggles to a new form of capitalism. This new form involved state intervention in the economy to regulate the market and redistribute wealth downward through social welfare and other state policies.

The new form has been referred to variously as New Deal capitalism, welfare capitalism, social democracy, or, in more technical terms, Fordism-Keynesianism. Regardless of what we name it, this state regulation of the market, redistributive policies, and working-class power acted as what we call "countervailing tendencies" to the tendency toward overaccumulation, that is, they helped offset overaccumulation. State intervention in the capitalist market and a component of redistribution came to define economic policy in the mid–twentieth century in the then First World, as well as in the then Third World in the wake of decolonization. This redistributive nation-state capitalism evolved, therefore, from capital's accommodation to mass upheavals from below in the wake of the crisis of the two world wars and the Great Depression. Capitalist classes had little choice but to accept these arrangements in the face of mass struggles, including socialist and communist movements, militant trade unionism, and anticolonial and Third World liberation movements. In any event, capital was able to sustain a high rate of profit for several decades as the world economy experienced an unprecedented boom in the aftermath of World War II and the devastation that it left in its wake.

As world capitalism entered its next structural crisis in the 1970s, capitalists and bureaucratic elites from around the world strove to beat back the power of organized labor, radical social movements, and Third World liberation struggles. These emerging transnationally oriented elites sought to win government during the 1980s and 1990s, typically through elections that took place on the heels of financial turmoil,[10] and to utilize state power to open up the world in new ways to transnational capital. In this way, reorganizing the system on a global scale became a strategy to reconstitute the power of capital over the working and popular classes, whose struggles remained at the level of the nation-state. As they went global, these capitalist groups integrated with one another across borders in pursuit of their collective class interests in a process of transnational class formation. A transnational capitalist class (TCC) emerged in this way as the manifest agent of global capitalism, about which much has been written by myself and others in recent years.[11] While there is intense competition within its own ranks, the members of this TCC share an interest in promoting global rather than national markets and circuits of accumulation, in competition with local and national capitalist groups and elites whose fate is more closely bound up with their particular nation-states and regions. By the end of the twentieth century, this TCC became the *hegemonic fraction of capital on a world scale*. It is made up of the owners and managers of the giant transnational corporations (TNCs) and financial institutions that drive the global economy. As the hegemonic fraction of capital, transnational capital increasingly integrates local circuits into its own; it imposes the general direction and character on production worldwide and conditions the social, political, and cultural character of capitalist society worldwide.

The unprecedented concentration of capital at the global level allowed the emerging transnational corporate elite to accumulate an enormous amount of power and control. The TCC and the states whose policies they were able to shape used this power to bring about a vast restructuring of the global economy and society, putting in place a new globally integrated production and financial system, as I will return to in the next chapter.[12] In this way, globalization made it possible for this TCC to increasingly break free of nation-state constraints to accumulation, such as the need to assure the reproduction of their own national proletariats, to do away with the model of redistributive nation-state capitalism and to beat back the tide of revolution in the Third World. This should have come as no surprise, as capitalist crises generally provide capitalists and the state with opportunities to restore profitability and push forward accumulation—although we must stress that these crises also open up new opportunities for counterhegemonic projects from below, as I shall discuss in chapter three.

Structural crises like those of the 1930s and the 1970s typically involve the transformation of patterns of capital accumulation and new rounds of expansion, often incorporating new cutting-edge technologies, such as the synthetic materials, consumer durables, automotive and petrochemicals, and military-industrial technologies that drove the post–World War II boom. Early in the twentieth century, the Soviet economist Nikolai Kondratieff noted how the world economy, driven by new cutting-edge technologies, experiences cycles of some forty to fifty years (called Kondratieff waves). In these cycles, rounds of expansion eventually become exhausted and are followed by downturns and crises, resulting in a reorganization of the system and new technologies that help launch a new cycle. However, the underlying causal dynamic that drives these cycles forward is the struggle among contending social and class forces. New Deal and social democratic arrangements, together with world war and the postwar expansion, "resolved" the structural crisis of the 1930s. But the contradictions internal to the model of redistributive nation-state capitalism led to a new structural crisis in the 1970s, as I mentioned above. The emerging TCC "resolved" this next structural crisis through sweeping worldwide economic restructuring made possible above all by new computer and information technologies.

In my view, the Great Recession of 2008 marked a new structural crisis that was not caused but became greatly aggravated by the pandemic. This crisis takes place under circumstances distinct from earlier ones. The economic and social disaster unleashed by the pandemic rivals that of the 1930s Great Depression, but the world capitalist system of today looks different than that of the early twentieth century. People and nations around the world have been linked into a single and constantly expanding world market since capitalism's inception in that symbolic year of 1492. In the five centuries that it has conquered the world, capitalism has gone through successive phases or epochs in its ongoing and open-ended evolution. Globalization ushered in a new epoch in world capitalism, characterized above all by the rise of a globally integrated production, financial, and service system under the control of the leading capitalist groups from around the world and their political agents in states. Indeed, the meltdown triggered by the pandemic highlighted just how dependent all countries have become on this globally integrated system. The nexus that links together all peoples and nations has dramatically tightened; in fact, it appears inextricable. It is the global networks of trade and travel that account for the rapidity with which the coronavirus spread around the world, as well as why it was so difficult to control through the action of individual states in a piecemeal fashion.[13] Now, the structural crises that started in 2008 and has become greatly aggravated by the pandemic is resulting, once again, in a sweeping restructuring and transformation of global capitalism, as we will explore in the next chapter.

Capitalist globalization and neoliberal austerity since the late 1970s pushed the global working and popular classes onto the defensive and shifted the global balance of class forces in favor of transnational capital following the period of mass struggles in the 1960s and 1970s. By liberating emergent transnational capital from national constraints, globalization undermined the redistributive programs that had attenuated capitalism's inherent tendency toward social polarization and had helped ensure the system's survival, at least for a while. The result has been an unprecedented sharpening of inequality that has fueled overaccumulation. Social polarization, to reiterate, is not an aberration under capitalism; it is its sine qua non. Marx showed in *Capital* how social polarization and inequality are inherent to the capitalist system, since capitalists own the means of producing wealth and, therefore, appropriate as profits as much of the wealth that society collectively produces as possible. In fact, the terms *pauper* (a Latin word meaning *in the character of a poor person*) and *pauperization* became popularized in our contemporary vocabulary as eighteenth-century industrial capitalism generated a new type of poverty that involved large groups of people uprooted from their traditional livelihoods and thrown into chronic impoverishment.

The level of global social polarization and inequality now experienced is without precedent. In 2018, the richest 1 percent of humanity controlled more than half of the world's wealth, while the bottom 80 percent had to make do with just 5 percent.[14] Such inequality ends up undermining the stability of the system as the gap grows between what is (or could be) produced and what the market can absorb. The extreme concentration of the planet's wealth in the hands of the few and the accelerated impoverishment and dispossession of the majority meant that transnational capital had increasing difficulty in finding productive outlets to unload the enormous amounts of surplus it had accumulated. The more global inequalities expand, the more constricted the world market becomes and the more the system faces a structural crisis of overaccumulation. If left unchecked, expanding social polarization results in crisis—in stagnation, recessions, depressions, social upheavals, and war—just what we are experiencing at this time.

As I noted above, the tendency for the rate of profit to fall and for capital to overaccumulate is just that—a tendency that can be offset, temporarily at least, by what are called countervailing tendencies and by mechanisms that may counteract the tendency. Frenzied financial speculation, unsustainable debt, the plunder of public finance, and state-organized militarized accumulation are just some of the mechanisms that the TCC and capitalist states turned to in the years leading up to the pandemic to keep the global economy sputtering along in the face of chronic stagnation. As the productive economy has stagnated, capitalists have turned above all to financial speculation.[15] The global economy has become a giant casino for transnational investors. In the wake of the Great Recession of 2008 the US Federal Reserve undertook a whopping $16 trillion in secret bailouts to banks and corporations around the world.[16] Then the banks and institutional investors simply recycled the trillions of dollars they received into new speculative activities in global commodities markets, in cryptocurrencies, and in land around the world, fueling a new global "land grab." As opportunity dried up for speculative investment in one sector, the TCC simply turned to another sector to unload its surplus. As a result, the gap between the productive economy and fictitious capital has grown into an enormous chasm.

Fictitious capital refers to money thrown into circulation without any base in commodities or production.[17] A major portion of the income generated by financial speculation is fictitious, meaning (here in simplified form) that it exists on paper but does not correspond to real wealth in the world, that is, goods and services that people need and want, such as food, clothing, houses, and so on. A company may for instance issue shares on the stock market that may be bought and sold by traders, but these shares do not correspond to the actual production of new wealth and typically become one of innumerable sources of financial speculation. Mortgages represent a claim on future rent, government bonds represent a claim on future tax revenue, derivative trading in futures markets represents claims on future values of commodities, and so on. The trade in this fictitious capital represents less the creation of new value or expanded production than the mirage of a bustling economy, as stock markets surge, assets values inflate, and credit expands. The accumulation of fictitious capital through speculation may offset the crisis temporally into the future or spatially to new digital geographies and new population groups but, in the long run, only exacerbates the underlying problem of overaccumulation. In 2018, for example, the gross world product, or the total value of goods and services, stood at some $75 trillion, whereas the global derivatives market—a marker of speculative activity—was estimated at a mind-boggling $1.2 quadrillion.[18] This accumulation of fictitious capital gave the appearance of recovery in the years following Great Recession of 2008, but it only offset the crisis temporally into the future, while in the long run exacerbating the underlying problem.

In addition to speculation, mounting government, corporate, and consumer debt drove growth in the first two decades of the twenty-first century. Consumer credit has served the dual purpose of class pacification, as workers and the poor are able to cover essential necessities for the moment, even as they become ever more indebted, and of generating demand, even as real incomes have dropped for the immiserated majority subject to austerity and ever more precarious forms of employment. In countries around the world, consumer debt was higher on the eve of the pandemic than it has been for all of postwar history. State and corporate debt also reached breaking points. The global bond market—an indicator of total government debt worldwide—more than doubled between 2003 and 2019, when it surpassed $105 trillion, while total global debt reached a staggering $258 trillion in 2020.[19] Particularly troubling is the growth of debt in the former Third World. The total debt for the thirty largest countries in the former Third World surpassed $72 trillion in 2019, a 168 percent rise over the previous decade. Worldwide corporate debt has soared to $75 trillion, up from $32 trillion in 2005, while, by 2018, corporations had issued $13 trillion in bonds, more than twice the bond debt on the eve of the 2008 collapse.[20]

Debt levels have soared through policies known as "quantitative easing," which essentially means that government treasuries print money and inject it into the banking system as cheap credit—even involving negative interest rates—in what some have referred to as "crack cocaine for financial markets." Quantitative easing ends up creating mountains of debt that sooner or later must collapse. A major default on consumer, state, or corporate debt—or waves of defaults—would set off a further chain reaction in the downward plunge of the global economy. The following table on the steep rise of fiat money—which refers to government-issued currency that is not backed by a commodity—shows the explosive growth of the money supply through quantitative easing that has aggravated the gap between fictitious capital and the real economy since 2008. Apart from the prospect of collapse itself, the out-of-control printing of money may in the long run trigger uncontrolled inflation that would further destabilize the global economy.

The TCC has also set out to raid and sack public finance, which has been reconfigured through austerity programs, bailouts, corporate subsidies, government debt, and the global bond market, as governments transfer wealth directly and indirectly from working people to the TCC. The global bond market itself serves as a vehicle to transfer wealth from the working classes to capital. Governments issue bonds to investors to close government budget deficits and also to subsidize private accumulation, so as to keep the economy going. They then have to pay back these bonds (with interest) by extracting

Fiat Money Quantity (FMQ) $bn

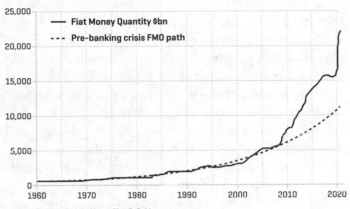

Source: St Louis Fed database (Fred), Goldmoney

taxes from current and future wages of the working classes. Already by the late twentieth century state income brought in by bonds often went right back to creditors. Thus, the reconfiguration of state finances amounts over time to a transfer of wealth from global labor to transnational capital: a claim by transnational capital on future wages, and a shift in the burden of the crisis to the working and popular classes. Yet financial pillage cannot resolve the crisis of overaccumulation and ends up aggravating it in the long run, as the transfer of wealth from workers to the TCC further constricts the market.

The ruling groups must not only figure out how to keep accumulating capital in the face of stagnation. They must also maintain control by keeping a lid on rebellion. As protest spreads around the world, they have turned to expanding the global police state, particularly in the aftermath of the pandemic, as the structural crisis becomes aggravated and as there is a further breakdown of capitalist hegemony. *Global police state* refers in the first instance to systems of transnational social control and repression to contain the oppressed. Savage global inequalities are politically explosive, and to the extent that the system is simply unable to reverse them or to incorporate surplus humanity it turns to ever more violent forms of containment to manage immiserated populations. As popular discontent has spread in recent years, the dominant groups have expanded transnational systems of social control, repression, and warfare—from mass incarceration to deadly new modalities of policing and omnipresent systems of state and private surveillance—to contain the actual and the potential rebellion of the global working class and surplus humanity.

Apart from political considerations, as I showed in my 2020 study *The Global Police State*, the global economy is becoming ever more dependent on the development and deployment of these systems of warfare, social control, and repression simply as a means of making profit and continuing to accumulate capital in the face of stagnation. This is what I refer to as *militarized accumulation* or *accumulation by repression*. The so-called wars on drugs and terrorism, the undeclared wars on immigrants, refugees, and gangs (and poor, dark-skinned, and working-class youth more generally), the construction of border walls, immigrant detention centers, prison-industrial complexes, systems of mass surveillance, and the spread of private security guard and mercenary companies have all become major sources of profit-making, and they will become more important to the system as stagnation becomes the new normal.

The events of September 11, 2001, marked the start of an era of a permanent global war in which logistics, warfare, intelligence, repression, surveillance, and even military personnel are more and more the privatized domain of transnational capital. The Pentagon budget increased 91 percent in real terms between 1998 and 2011, while, worldwide, total defense outlays grew by 50 percent from 2006 to 2015, from $1.4 trillion to $2.03 trillion, although this figure does not take into account hundreds of billions of dollars in "homeland security" spending. In the decade from 2001 to 2011, military industry profits nearly quadrupled.[21] Led by the United

States as the predominant world power, military expansion in different countries has taken place through parallel, and often conflictive, processes, yet all show the same relationship between state militarization and global capital accumulation. Worldwide, official state military outlays in 2015 represented about 3 percent of the gross world product of $75 trillion.

Militarized accumulation involves vastly more than activities generated by state military budgets. There are immense sums involved in state spending and private corporate accumulation through militarization and other forms of generating profit through repressive social control that do not involve militarization per se. The various wars, conflicts, and campaigns of social control and repression around the world involve the fusion of private accumulation with state militarization. In this relationship, the state facilitates the expansion of opportunities for private capital to accumulate through militarization, such as by facilitating global weapons sales by military-industrial-security firms, the amounts of which have reached unprecedented levels. Global weapons sales by the top one hundred weapons manufacturers and military service companies increased by 38 percent between 2002 and 2016.[22]

By 2018, private military companies employed some fifteen million people around the world, deploying forces to guard corporate property, providing personal security for TCC executives and their families, collecting data, conducting police, paramilitary, counterinsurgency, and surveillance operations, carrying out mass crowd control and repression of protesters, managing prisons, running private detention and interrogation facilities, and participating in outright warfare.[23] The private security (policing) business is one of the fastest growing economic sectors in many countries and has come to dwarf public security around the world. The amount spent on private security in 2003, the year of the invasion of Iraq, was 73 percent higher than that spent in the public sphere, and three times as many persons were employed in private forces as in official law enforcement agencies. There were an outstanding twenty million private security workers worldwide in 2017, and the industry was expected to be worth over $220 billion by 2020. In half of the world's countries, private security agents outnumber police officers.[24]

In the end, financial speculation, pillaging the state, and debt-driven growth are all temporary "fixes" that cannot address the underlying structural conditions that have thrown the world economy into crisis. The massive concentrations of transnational finance capital destabilized the system as global capitalism ran up against the limits of these fixes. The expansion of a global war economy may pick up some of the slack, but it has its limits and is not in the long run a viable solution. Moreover, such an economy generates and is generated by acute political and military conflict that destabilizes the system. The global economy was a ticking time bomb. All that was needed was something to light the fuse. That came in the form of the Covid-19 pandemic.

...AND THEN THE PANDEMIC

The origins of Covid-19 remain in dispute. The evidence that the virus displays "gain of function" (GOF) properties is considerable. It is feasible that it was developed in a biolab and *accidentally* leaked out. (For that matter, the development of the virus as an agent of biological warfare cannot be ruled out. The United States, Israel, China, and Russia are some of the countries known to have bioweapon research programs, and the Pentagon alone operates biowarfare laboratories in twenty-five countries around the world).[25] Given the contemporary proliferation of unfounded conspiracy theories, we must stress that the possibility the virus was developed in a laboratory *in no way implies that it would have been intentionally leaked or that there was a larger plot to cause a pandemic*. Rather, the forensics of the virus, as well as the social and political response to the outbreak, must be subject to critical analysis given the likelihood of new and deadlier pandemics in the future.

Among those who identified the virus's GOF properties and argued that it was created in a laboratory was the 2008 Nobel laureate for Medicine Luc Montagnier, a French virologist who first discovered the HIV virus.[26] GOF research attempts to combat potentially deadly microbes proactively by first creating them artificially in a laboratory in order to develop a vaccine against them, in a process known as "biosynthesis" (see next chapter). In 2011, the Erasmus Medical Center in Rotterdam announced at a European scientific conference that it had found a way to turn H5N1, a coronavirus that almost exclusively infected birds, into a possible human-to-human flu. Researcher Ron Fouchier told the gathered scientists that the Dutch research team, with funding from the US National Institute of Health, had "mutated the hell out of H5N1," turning the bird flu into a variant that could infect ferrets, a laboratory stand-in for human beings.[27]

The claims that Covid-19 originated in a biolab, possibly even at the US Army's Medical Research Institute of Infectious Diseases at Fort Detrick in Maryland,[28] cannot be dismissed as "conspiracy theory," because there is enough credible evidence to make that plausible. A conspiracy is a plot by two or more actors to undertake some action toward an intended outcome. Conspiracies, therefore, take place routinely as part of the natural course of human affairs. Theories about conspiracies should be dismissed when they are not backed by verifiable evidence; well-documented conspiracies cease to be theories. "Regimes of truth," as French philosopher Michel Foucault put it, distinguish between acceptable and unacceptable ideas. They set the boundaries of acceptable discourse as established by power dynamics.[29]

There are plenty of wild and baseless conspiracy theories circulating among the public, often associated with the far right, such as the claim that Jews or the Illuminati are plotting to take over the world.[30] Notwithstanding, the pejorative charge of "conspiracy theory" is all too readily evoked by those in position of power to dismiss arguments that may be threatening to their interests or contrary to acceptable narratives. It is remarkable given the widely available evidence that should lead journalists and researchers to at the very least retain skepticism regarding the official narrative on the origin of the novel Covid-19 coronavirus that the *New York Times*, among others, simply dismissed any but this official narrative as "unfounded conspiracy theory."[31] As part of our training, scientists—social as much as natural—learn that we cannot ignore empirical evidence simply because by not ignoring it we are subject to reprobation by the powers that be, or because our funders cut off support if that evidence contravenes official accounts.

Here is what we do know. Biosafety Level 3 and 4 laboratories have proliferated around the world in recent years, and their research includes developing new strains of microbes, including viruses, along with vaccines to immunize people from them. Prior to the Covid-19 outbreak, the global vaccine market was valued at over $40 billion and projected to increase to nearly $60 billion by 2024.[32] The US government's Defense Advanced Research Projects Agency (DARPA) had been researching coronaviruses and bats prior to the Covid-19 outbreak. Once the pandemic hit, it set out to develop a vaccine for the virus in collaboration with leading pharmaceutical companies, and with the participation of the World Health Organization, the Bill and Melinda Gates Foundation (one of the largest benefactors of the WHO), the World Economic Forum, and several other governments.[33] As with other United Nations agencies, the WHO used to be funded principally by states, but as rich states have cut funding to the WHO and other agencies, transnational corporations and the philanthropies ("philanthro-capitalists") they endow have become major funders (in 2020, about 70 percent of the WHO's budget came from private donations). Thus, the TCC can bypass the mediation of states and directly shape the WHO's policies.

In shaping global health policies through the WHO and private channels, the TCC has sought to privatize public health systems and to open up new opportunities for accumulation by the medical and pharmaceutical industry. This effort includes the creation of global markets for vaccines and other drugs developed by pharmaceutical corporations. As has been well documented, the Bill and Melinda Gates Foundation has been at the forefront of these efforts. Dutch international relations scholar Kees van der Pijl noted in a 2020 paper that "health has been a key concern of the $52 billion Gates Foundation (and of the Rockefeller Foundation for that matter) and Bill Gates has pursued his private views on a grand scale as a result." As part of its campaign to privatize and commodify health and educational systems around the world, in the years prior to the pandemic the Gates Foundation funded a series of vaccine programs, some of them highly controversial, in collaboration with leading global pharmaceutical corporations, and has pushed for mandatory vaccination laws, with the goal of expanding global markets for the industry.[34] "[If] we could stimulate the pharmaceutical companies through public private partnerships to create vaccines," explained Melinda Gates in 2012, "if we could guarantee them a market of millions of children getting this vaccine and then being paid for it in the developing world. If we could commit to a market and we knew that the demand would be there, we could incent them with the right research dollars to actually create those vaccines."[35] Once the coronavirus pandemic hit, the foundation enlisted these corporations, rather than public laboratories and health systems, to develop a vaccine, assuring that the response to the pandemic would be driven by the pursuit of private profit.[36] Among the beneficiaries of the foundation's multibillion-dollar tax-deductible donations to private companies were leading pharmaceutical corporations and the private hospital industry that stood to cash in on the sale of billions of test kits, therapeutic treatments, and vaccines, with the foundation owning stocks and bonds in these corporations.[37]

As we shall explore in the next chapter, the pharmaceutical industry has not been the only one to benefit from the pandemic. Governments around the world reached out to tech platforms for help with enforcing quarantines and public gathering restrictions. In the United States, Facebook and Google met with Trump administration officials to discuss drafting the phone data of US residents into a system of heightened surveillance in the name of fighting the virus, while Amazon unveiled a program to deliver test kits and test Seattle area residents in partnership with the Bill and Melinda Gates Foundation.[38] Shortly after the pandemic hit, Gates suggested issuing universal "digital certificates" for each member of the public attesting to the bearer's coronavirus and vaccine status.[39] Mass vaccination against coronavirus may well have been necessary from a public health perspective, although the matter was not without controversy. The point here is that the pandemic presented the global pharmaceutical industry with a potential windfall. Once the virus spread, developing a vaccine became an imperative from the viewpoint of public health. A global race to develop a vaccine pit open sourcing against corporate control through patent monopoly. With the stakes so high, Amnesty International warned against global vaccine apartheid, urging that "Big Pharma profits must not be prioritized over the health of billions"[40]

Hence, to reiterate, the way that the pandemic was exploited for other purposes became far more important than the forensics of the event itself.[41] Rather than a plan hatched beforehand to achieve the desired outcome, powerful political and corporate actors seized upon the pandemic to advance an agenda, elements of which had been gestating and others improvised later. "Once the health emergency opportunity presented itself, the pharmaceutical industry was obviously first in line to defend, not just a capitalist response, but also a specific medication-oriented approach to health," observed van der Pijl. He noted that Bill Gates and the World Health Organization that he finances had long called for pandemic preparedness. "The dress rehearsals more than the actual Covid-19 crisis determined the response, to which the other IT giants, high finance, and the intelligence/surveillance world added their weight." He further observed, "A paralyzed society will not resist the shock-like acceleration of the concentration of capital in fewer hands either."[42]

It is well-documented that at least a decade ahead of the outbreak, scenarios for such a pandemic were rehearsed. A 2010 report by the Rockefeller Foundation described a "Lockstep Scenario" that would start with a coronavirus pandemic. In this scenario, the pandemic would result in "a world of tighter top-down government control and more authoritarian leadership, with limited innovation and growing citizen pushback." The conclusion reached by some that the report proves the pandemic was planned is entirely unsubstantiated and unwarranted—claims to that extent end up undermining legitimate critique of how capitalist states launched particular strategies for dealing with the pandemic compatible with the interests of the TCC. Of concern to us here, the uncanny report envisioned that the scenario would drive a dramatic expansion of state control and digitally driven technologies:

> China's government was not the only one that took extreme measures to protect its citizens from risk and exposure. During the pandemic, national leaders around the world flexed their authority and imposed airtight rules and restrictions, from the mandatory wearing of face masks to body-temperature checks at the entries to communal spaces like train stations

and supermarkets. Even after the pandemic faded, this more authoritarian control and oversight of citizens and their activities stuck and even intensified. In order to protect themselves from the spread of increasingly global problems—from pandemics and transnational terrorism to environmental crises and rising poverty— leaders around the world took a firmer grip on power.[43]

Then on the eve of the pandemic, the World Economic Forum, the Johns Hopkins University Center for Health Security, and Gates Foundation held a symposium in New York, "Event-201—A Global Pandemic Exercise," as a large-scale simulation. Dubbed a "germ-game," based on a fictional scenario in which a coronavirus that jumped from pigs to humans spread around the world, the exercise laid out a plan for corporate domination of any response to a potential pandemic, including the suppression of any narratives that might contradict official ones. Presaging what would actually take place during the pandemic, the exercise recommended that "governments, international organizations, and businesses" should plan for "how essential corporate capabilities will be utilized during a large-scale pandemic." It recommended that governments partner with private media corporations to develop "the ability to flood media with fast, accurate, and consistent information... trusted, influential private-sector employers should create the capacity to readily and reliably augment public messaging, manage rumors and misinformation, and amplify credible information to support emergency public communications... media companies should commit to ensuring that authoritative messages are prioritized and that false messages are suppressed including through the use of technology."[44]

As I stated above, I am not in a position to review and evaluate the mass of contending accounts and their merits with regard to verifiable evidence. What concerns us here is that whether an accidental release from a biolab or simply a transmission from bats to humans in a Chinese wet market *the effects are the same*: a global health emergency that facilitated a massive transfer of wealth to the rich and allowed the ruling classes to impose a state of exception, enhance surveillance and control through the global police state, and accelerate the restructuring of global capitalism through a new wave of digital technologies. As we shall see in the next chapter, the pandemic was a boon to the leading sectors of capital worldwide, led by the tech sector, interwoven as it is with finance, pharmaceuticals, and the military-industrial complex. Powerful political actors seized on the health emergency to manipulate fear of contagion, in the words of researcher Piers Robinson, "fully aware that these conditions of fear and panic provide a critical opportunity that can be exploited in order to pursue political, economic, and societal objectives."[45] Robinson, van der Pijl, and others were quick to note parallels between the aftermath of the September 11, 2001, attacks on the World Trade Center and the Pentagon and the state of exception imposed around the world as the coronavirus spread. As with September 2001, the emergency mobilization, perhaps necessary from a public health point of view, provided the conditions for a new wave of control by the corporate and political agents of global capitalism.

THE VIRAL PANDEMIC AND THE PANDEMIC OF CAPITALISM

The coronavirus may not have been caused—directly—by global capitalism, but it did pull back the veil of a global capitalist system that had been wreaking calamity on the poor majority of humanity long before the outbreak began. The pandemic left in its wake more inequality, more political tension, more militarism, and more authoritarianism—or, rather, there were more of these things *through* the pandemic. Capitalist states around the world, unable to cope with the pandemic and the fallout from the socioeconomic implosion it triggered, were exposed as callous instruments of wealth and corruption, aggravating many times over the political dimension of global capitalist crisis, that of state legitimacy and capitalist hegemony. Just as with everything else that occurs in society, the pandemic did not unfold on its own terms but in the context of capitalist society, driven above all by the implacable logic of accumulation and on the terrain of all the existing relations of power, inequality, and oppression. The pandemic, therefore, was not solely a biomedical phenomenon. It was as much social as economic, political, and environmental. Its impacts were integral to ongoing processes of domination and resistance, and, as we shall see in the next chapter, these impacts also accelerated a new wave of restructuring and transformation of global capitalism.

The class character of the health emergency could not have been clearer. The virus did not care about the class, ethnicity, or nationality of the human hosts it sought to infect, but it was the poor and working classes who were unable to protect themselves from contagion, and whose conditions put them at much greater risk. As is known, those with poor health to begin with or with preexisting medical conditions were most susceptible to falling ill, and, if ill, to dying from the virus. Those with poor health and preexisting risk factors were the most likely to have inadequate access to health care, to live in congested circumstances and in substandard housing, to have inadequate access to nutritious food, and to work in jobs that are hazardous and in areas with elevated exposure to environmental toxins. In the teeming slums of the world's megacities, social distancing was a privilege that was out of reach. Millions became ill, and many died, not so much from the viral infection as from the lack of access to life-sustaining services and resources.[46]

International agencies warned early in the pandemic of the devastating impact it would have on the world's poor majority. Even before the pandemic hit, the number of those experiencing hunger and food insecurity was rising. In 2019, some 1.5 billion people suffered from hunger and severe levels of food insecurity, another 500 million did not have access to nutritious and sufficient food.[47] An April 2020 report by the international development agency Oxfam warned that the pandemic would push an additional half a billion people into poverty and threatened to set poor regions such as sub-Saharan Africa and the Middle East back thirty years in terms of their development. "Existing inequalities dictate the economic impact of this crisis," said the report. "The poorest workers in rich and poor nations are less likely to be in formal employment, enjoy labor protections such as sick pay, or be able to work from home." It went on to note that women, who make up 70 percent of health workers globally and provide 75 percent of unpaid care of children, the sick, and the elderly, were at the front line of the coronavirus response and were the hardest hit financially.[48]

The momentary lull in the global economy in the opening months of the pandemic brought respite to heavily polluted cities and waterways. In the canals of Venice, water became crystal clear, and fish could be seen for the first time in memory. Almost surreal scenes spread around the world of deer and other wildlife roaming deserted city streets during lockdowns. Air pollution that normally chokes millions seemed to magically disappear for a few fleeting months. These changes gave us a glimpse of what a radical transformation of the global political economy could achieve for the environment. Yet the respite in pollution was short-lived. Within months, it became clear that the climate emergency was on track to intensify even in the midst of the pandemic. The fall 2020 hurricane season in the Caribbean and the Pacific, the most severe on record, wreaked devastation on Central America. Months earlier, California was wracked by unprecedented wildfires that raged uncontrolled. A record heat wave in Siberia marked a dramatic acceleration of permafrost loss and left millions of people on unstable ground. The European Environmental Agency warned that the increased use of single-use plastics and the sharp rise in the generation of household waste brought about by the pandemic posed a significant environmental risk that would continue into the future as the spread of viral and bacterial infections increased and as new pandemics loomed.[49]

In the larger picture, the pandemic itself was an outcome of the environmental crisis, which in turn is driven by global capitalism, with its implacable logic of accumulation. Scientists and epidemiologists had been warning of a pandemic for at least a decade before the Covid-19 outbreak.[50] Human and livestock encroachment on animal habitats, deforestation, the extension of farming driven by the expansion of transnational agribusiness, logging, mining, and factory farms, and the resulting urbanization, climate change, and pollution, bring society into increasing proximity with formerly isolated ecosystems and create multiple bridges for microbes to leap from wild animals to humans, either directly or through animals confined to factory farms.[51] Sixty percent of human infectious diseases are of animal origin and three-fourths of new diseases are transmitted from animals, including viruses responsible for significant global mortality, such as the HIV-1 and HIV-2 viruses, the Rift Valley fever virus, and influenza viruses, such as bird flus and swine flus.[52] In fact, over the past fifty years zoonotic diseases—that is, those that spread from animals to humans—have quadrupled.[53] Rising global temperatures favor the development and spread of infectious diseases. They also extend the scope of transmission of diseases to new zones. As regions previously too cold for malaria heat up, for instance, they will become susceptible to the mosquito-borne disease. As permafrost in arctic and subarctic regions melts, there is concern over the release of bacteria and viruses that have so far remained frozen, and for which humans would have little immune resistance.

Capital wasted no time in endeavoring to shift the burden of the crisis and the sacrifice that the pandemic imposed onto the working and popular classes. The ruling classes set out to push policies to exploit every aspect of the pandemic for private profit. "Never let a crisis go to waste" was how US president Barack Obama's chief of staff Rahm Emanuel famously put it during the 2008 financial collapse. For this purpose, it could count on capitalist state power. Many governments turned to massive new bailouts of capital with only very modest relief, if any at all, for the working classes. The US government injected an initial $1.5 trillion into Wall Street banks, with the White House promising that its response to the pandemic is "centered fully on unleashing the power of the private sector,"[54] meaning that capitalist profit would come first and would shape the response to the emergency. It then passed several other multitrillion-dollar stimulus packages, the single biggest component of which was a giveaway to corporations along with smaller amounts for relief to the unemployed and poor families (early on in the pandemic, the US Federal Reserve was buying $1 million in financial assets *every second*).[55]

In Europe, the EU and member governments approved similar stimulus packages,[56] as did the Chinese government.[57] The US and EU governments provided an astonishing eight-trillion-dollar handout to private corporations in the first two months of the pandemic alone, an amount roughly equivalent to their profits over the preceding two years.[58] Most governments around the world approved packages that involved the same combination of fiscal stimulus, corporate bailout, and modest public relief, if any.[59] One report showed that 2.7 billion people around the world received no government support whatsoever to cope with the pandemic.[60] Even if deficit spending and Keynesian stimulus were to remain in place for the duration of a depression, the experience of 2008 showed that governments recovered the costs of bailouts by deepening social austerity, even as banks and corporations used bailout money to buy back stock and engage in new rounds of predatory activities.

As savage as global inequalities already were, the wealth gap widened rapidly around the world during the pandemic. Assisted by corporate bailouts, in the United States, the ultra-wealthy increased their wealth by $931 billion from March to October 2020, even as sixty million workers lost their jobs, and as poverty, hunger, and homelessness spread.[61] Worldwide, billionaires' wealth jumped by 27 percent, to $10.2 trillion in just four months of the pandemic, from April to June 2020, according to a report by the Swiss bank UBS, which also warned against the threat of a global uprising by the poor against the superrich.[62] The pockets of the rich were also lined through pandemic price gouging, reflecting a gangster capitalism based ever more on fraud, racketeering, and crime in high places.[63] In the midst of the pandemic, the US-based news service BuzzFeed published an exposé on widespread criminal operations at the highest level at Deutsche Bank, one of the largest banks in the world.[64] In the United States, private hospitals, owned for the most part by corporate hospital systems, jacked up charges to patients by as much as eighteen times above costs. These corporate hospitals, according to one study, charged from $1,129 to $1,808 for every $100 of their costs, as the industry's profits approached an annual rate of $100 billion.[65]

As the rich got richer, there were no mass bailouts for the billions of poor precarious and informal sector workers, whose daily struggles for survival suddenly became a near unsurmountable challenge. The International Labour Organization (ILO) predicted in mid-March 2020 that 25 million people worldwide would lose their jobs as a result of the virus.[66] One month later, the ILO warned that *nearly half the global workforce* was at risk, including 305 million workers with full-time jobs, and 1.6 billion workers in the informal sector. The agency estimated that as a result of economic closures and lockdowns informal sector workers globally faced a drop of 60 percent of income; 81 percent in Africa and the Americas, 21.6 percent in Asia and the Pacific, and 70 percent in Europe and Central

Asia.[67] In Latin America, 34 million people lost their jobs due
to the pandemic, according to the ILO, or some 20 percent of
the region's workforce—a rate nearly double the 12 percent
job loss worldwide.[68] But as the pandemic stretched into 2021,
the ILO had to continuously up its estimates of the number
of people thrown into unemployment. In January of that year,
it reported that 255 million workers worldwide had lost their
jobs.[69] As I will discuss in the next chapter, some of those made
unemployed may be absorbed back into the workforce, but
under new post-pandemic work conditions involving much
greater discipline, alienation, and exploitation.

As elsewhere around the world, however, official job loss
tells only a small portion of the story, given that some two
billion people labor in the informal sector, meaning that they
are not among those formally employed (this held true also
for those tens, or perhaps hundreds, of millions in the rich
countries who are considered "self-employed" and outsourced
contract workers, even though they work for transnational
corporate employers, such as Uber drivers and grocery deliv-
erers). Some one billion children worldwide were affected
by school closures. Hundreds of millions of transnational
migrants and refugees faced the virus with no access to any
health infrastructure. Prisoners in overcrowded jails the world
over, the homeless, and those in war zones were sitting ducks
for the virus. The story of the contagion was a story of the
shocking disparities in the degree of risk to which different
social classes and groups were exposed—risk that became
overlaid onto already unprecedented levels of global inequality
going into the pandemic. As the worst of the pandemic passed
and economic malaise set in, the TCC strived to take advan-
tage of long-term mass unemployment and job insecurity to
attempt to enhance its class power over labor through further
discipline and austerity.

The global working class experienced the pandemic
through four structural locations. First were hundreds of

millions who shifted to telework, involving a very significant change in the nature of the labor process, as I will discuss in the next chapter. Second were "essential workers," frontline workers who were forced to continue working or felt the need to do so out of economic desperation—health care, warehouse and delivery, agriculture, meatpacking, food processing, and so on. The pandemic had a particularly devastating impact on these informal-sector and low-wage workers in essential industries and services. (In the United States, for instance, residents earning less than $20,000 annually were twice as likely to have lost their job as someone earning over $80,000 a year).[70] Workers deemed essential were often forced into dangerous work arrangements, such as health care workers, who had to labor with insufficient personal protective equipment. Third were those workers who lost their jobs (or were unemployed to begin with) and faced uncertain prospects of recovering employment post-pandemic. And forth were the mass of informal sector workers—two billion worldwide.

The crisis provided agents of the TCC in capitalist states and supranational organizations—what I have referred to as transnational state (TNS) apparatuses[71]—with a lever to force indebted countries in the former Third World into a new round of neoliberal reform. "Countries will need to implement structural reforms to help shorten the time to recovery," declared World Bank president David Malpass at a virtual meeting of the G20 finance ministers held in the midst of the pandemic. "For those countries that have excessive regulations, subsidies, licensing regimes, trade protection, or litigiousness as obstacles, we will work with them to foster markets, choice, and faster growth prospects during recovery," that is, to push to further liberate transnational capital from any state or popular class constraint.[72] The International Monetary Fund (IMF) launched a Covid-19 Financial Assistance and Debt Relief initiative, making available $1 trillion in new loans and temporarily suspending servicing of the debt owed to multilateral agencies.[73] The initiative, however, did not involve any debt forgiveness or suspend the accrual of interest, so that countries emerged from the pandemic more heavily indebted than going into it—this at a time when many countries experienced a sharp drop in foreign exchange receipts as commodity prices sunk, remittances from workers abroad sent home declined, and the world tourist industry nearly collapsed.

THE PANDEMIC AND THE GLOBAL POLICE STATE

Governments around the world centralized the response to the pandemic and many declared states of emergencies: in effect, imposing what some called "medical martial law." Such centralized coordination may have been justified as necessary to confront the health crisis, but centralization of emergency powers in authoritarian capitalist states was used to deploy police and military forces to contain discontent, heighten surveillance, and impose repressive social control—that is, to push forward the global police state. By May 2020, at least four billion people were under government lockdowns, more than the number of people in the world who have access to internet broadband, social media, or indoor safe toilet sanitation.[74]

As the world emerged from the contagion, states used what van der Pijl referred to as a "bio-political emergency" to further normalize and institutionalize state surveillance and repressive control in a way reminiscent of the aftermath of the 2001 attacks. In the wake of those attacks, 140 countries passed draconian "anti-terrorist" security legislation that often made legal the repression of social movements and political dissent. The laws remained in place long after the 2001 events. "The counterterror laws enacted around the globe represent a dangerous expansion of powers to detain and prosecute people, including peaceful political opponents," warned a 2012 report by Human Rights Watch. "The elements that raise grave human rights concerns include overly broad and vague definitions of terrorism—such as 'disrupting the public order'—as well as sweeping powers for warrantless search and arrest, the use of secret evidence, and immunity for police who abuse the laws."[75] As countries around the world raced to contain the pandemic, "many are deploying digital surveillance tools as a means to exert social control, even turning security agency technologies on their own civilians," noted one *New York Times* article, recalling the experience of 2001. Ratcheting up surveillance during an emergency "could permanently open the doors to more invasive forms of snooping later," the newspaper warned. "Law enforcement agencies have access to higher-powered surveillance systems, like fine-grained location tracking and facial recognition—technologies that may be repurposed to further political agendas like anti-immigration policies."[76]

In country after country, emergency powers were used to selectively ban protests on the grounds that they spread the virus, harass dissidents, censor journalists, and scapegoat minority groups. At least 158 governments imposed restrictions on demonstrations. At the very start of the pandemic in Wuhan, Chinese officials silenced doctors who first raised the alarm. In Egypt, at least twelve doctors were thrown in jail for criticizing the government response to the contagion. Many governments criminalized "fake news," which often meant reports that criticized the ruling groups. The Nicaraguan government criminalized *any* news reporting, pandemic or otherwise, that it deemed to "cause alarm, fear, or anxiety." In Zimbabwe, anyone who published or disseminated "false information" about an official or that the government deemed to impede its response to the pandemic was threatened with jail terms of up to twenty years. Bulgarian authorities imposed a harsher lockdown on Romany neighborhoods than on others. The Malaysian government blamed migrant workers for the virus, while a UN rapporteur charged the Myanmar/Burmese government with stepping up its repression of the Rohingyas and other ethnic minorities.[77] The Russian government demanded that the media stop publishing information on the virus that it declared to be false. The governments of Turkey, Montenegro, and Serbia carried out arrests and fined people who published information on social media that "provokes panic and jeopardizes public security."[78]

Throughout Europe, thousands of soldiers were deployed to quarantined cities to patrol streets and enforce lockdowns. Even the conservative weekly the *Economist* felt obliged to warn that "armed forces are designed first and foremost for killing people, rather than issuing fines on street corners or delivering food to supermarkets."[79] In Hungary, the far-right authoritarian prime minister Viktor Orban sought an open-ended state of emergency that would give him powers to bypass parliament and rule by decree.[80] One early April 2020 headline banner by the influential publication *Foreign Policy* declared, "Coronavirus and the Dawn of Post-Democratic Europe."[81] In Great Britain, a coronavirus bill was rushed through parliament that authorized the government to detain and isolate people indefinitely, to ban public gatherings, including protests, and to shut down ports and airports with little oversight.[82]

In the United States the national guard was activated in all fifty states (this happened *before* the anti-racist uprising in the wake of the May 2020 police murder of George Floyd), and the US Department of Justice secretly asked Congress to suspend constitutional rights during the health crisis, including the suspension of habeas corpus.[83] A law passed in New York State gave Governor Mario Cuomo unlimited authority to rule by executive order and overrule existing regulations during state crises like pandemics and hurricanes.[84] Several states enacted laws to criminalize protest against fossil fuels by designating them as "critical infrastructure."[85] The State of Oregon, among others, imposed a penalty of jail or a $1,200 fine or both for those who broke quarantine. President Donald Trump did not invoke the Defense Production Act, which authorizes the president to expedite and expand the supply of materials and services from the US industrial base in response to national defense and other emergencies, to manufacture personal protective equipment (PPE), which remained in critically short supply throughout most of 2020. Instead, he invoked the act to declare that meatpacking workers, many of whom were particularly vulnerable immigrants, were "essential," and to order them back to work under hazardous conditions. After workers were forced back to work at a Tyson Foods meat processing plant in April in the US state of Iowa, company supervisors and managers placed bets among themselves on how many employees would catch the virus. Within a month, one thousand workers had contracted the virus, and at least six of them died from complications.[86]

From Russia to Singapore to South Korea governments around the world stepped up surveillance of their populations as the virus became a testbed for surveillance capitalism. The Italian, German, Chinese, and Austrian governments, among others, put systems in place in coordination with the giant tech corporations as the disease spread to analyze smartphone data so as to determine to what extent populations were complying with the lockdown.[87] The Tunisian government deployed robocops—tank-like surveillance robots with facial recognition abilities—to patrol streets. One video posted to social media appeared to show one of the robots scanning a woman's papers. On the video, the woman is seen rummaging around her purse to produce papers.[88] Drones were deployed by authorities in some parts of the United States, Europe, Australia, China, and elsewhere to patrol lockdowns from the skies. The New York City police department deployed a fleet of drones to patrol Central Park in search of social-distance violators, while in Australia a mechanical voice emitted by drones that flashed the red and blue lights of police vehicles broadcast commands from the sky for locals to maintain social distancing at all times. The University of Southern Australia debuted drones manufactured by the Canadian-based Draganfly, a leading drone company, that had the ability to detect fever, cough, respiratory and heart rates, and blood pressure from a distance.[89]

Some countries required citizens to carry documents verifying their "right" to be out of their homes, even if, as in France, they could handwrite these documents themselves. The idea seems to have been merely to get populations accustomed to producing papers on demand, to ask permission to exist in public space. Even in those countries whose lockdowns did not require residents to carry paperwork to show permission to be out of home, one observer cautioned, "the conditioning still pointed toward a submissive permission-oriented model of domestic movement."[90] Australians had to choose between sixteen authorized "excuses" to be outdoors, while the UK government warned that being caught out of home "without a reasonable excuse" would trigger a fine that would double with every offense. In Italy, local governments captured location data transmitted by residents' mobile phones to determine who was obeying the lockdown order and the typical distances they moved each day.[91] In South Korea, government agencies harnessed surveillance camera footage, smartphone location data, and credit card purchases to trace the movements of those infected by the virus.

The dictatorial Kenyan government went much further, with police unleashing a wave of repression against citizens struggling their best to obey the lockdown. In downtown Nairobi, police whipped and kicked people on the street. In Embakasi, they forced people walking home from work to kneel before them, and in the port city of Mombasa, security forces teargassed crowds trying to board a ferry home, beating them with batons and gun butts, and then forced them to huddle together and lie on top of one another. At least thirty people were confirmed to have been killed in the state violence in the first six months of the pandemic.[92] In the Philippines, strong-man president Rodrigo Duterte issued shoot to kill orders for anyone defying the stay-at-home lockdown, while his government stepped up its campaign of extrajudicial killing of thousands of supposed criminals.[93] In Israel, the government's Shin Bet intelligence agency announced it would monitor cell phones for citizens' location data to surveil the movement of potentially infected individuals and contact trace them. Prime Minister Benjamin Netanyahu stated that the method of contact tracing would be the same that the government routinely used against "terrorists [read: Palestinians]."[94] In hundreds of cities in China, the government required citizens to use software on their phones that automatically classified each person with a color code—red, yellow, or green—indicating contagion risk and determining which people should be quarantined or permitted to enter public places like subways. At least thirty other countries issued such citizen tracking orders.[95]

In a least a dozen countries in Latin America, the armed forces were called out to enforce lockdowns against a labor force that in its majority works in the informal sector and could not survive staying at home. In Lima, Guatemala City, and elsewhere starving households had to wave white flags as if they were surrendering as they broke mandatory lockdowns in search of food and supplies. The Peruvian armed forces arrested more than eighteen thousand residents for violating the lockdown. The Salvadoran government similarly arrested thousands of people for violating home quarantine and locked them up in "containment centers" that lacked proper hygiene and safety requirements. In Bolivia, the government of Jeanine Añez, which came to power in an illegal coup d'état in October 2019, used the contagion as a pretext for mass repression of political opponents (Añez was forced to leave office after losing elections held in October 2020).[96] All over the region, charged Amnesty International, governments turned to "arbitrary, punitive and repressive tactics" to enforce compliance with quarantine measures and clamp down on popular protest. "Added to the structural challenges and massive social and economic divides present prior to the pandemic, these measures only combine to perpetuate inequality and discrimination across the continent."[97]

Honduras provided a case study in how the ruling groups used the health emergency to legitimate an escalation of state repression. The dictatorial regime, put into power by a US-backed coup d'état in 2009, ordered a nationwide lockdown enforced by the Honduran military and police. The lockdown included the suspension of numerous constitutional guarantees, including freedom of expression, freedom of movement, and freedom from arbitrary detention. Hundreds of arrests, some of them of known political dissidents, were carried out in the first few days of the order. A life and death situation spread across Honduras with the closure of street markets and roadside vendors. Some 60 percent of all Hondurans live in poverty, and a full 70 percent are employed in the informal sector. As in other countries around the world, confinement at home was simply not possible for this impoverished majority. The repressive lockdown meant that millions faced starvation, unable to go out in search of food, assistance, or other necessities for survival without risking military and police repression. The government used emergency funds to politicize food packages doled out to supporters of the ruling National Party. In several municipalities, residents who took to the streets to demand relief were met by bullets, tear gas, and arrests.[98]

The Indian government was particularly vicious in its declaration of a state of emergency and mandatory confinement at home. In what was arguably the world's strictest lockdown, hundreds of millions of precarious and informal workers who had no choice but to starve or leave home to scrape by were met with brutal and humiliating police violence, scenes of which were caught on televisions cameras and social media recordings and aired around the world. Tens of millions more migrant workers were caught by the lockdown far away from their villages. With public transportation shut down, they were forced to endure pitiless state repression as they marched hundreds of kilometers to get home. Media reports were full of stories of extreme dehumanization of these migrant workers, deaths in custody, mass arrests, and spraying people with bleach as a disinfectant. The state of Karnataka, in but one example, required all individuals during the lockdown to send in selfies of themselves at home every hour. Those who failed to do so, warned the government, would be sent to mass quarantine centers.[99] As the Indian government escalated its repression it targeted human rights organizations, forcing Amnesty International to close its offices in the country in September 2020.

There was little doubt that the pandemic allowed the ruling groups to further tighten the global police state. But it also allowed the TCC to consolidate its grip over the global economy, especially leading sectors of global capital that flourished during the pandemic, as we shall discuss in the next chapter. India provides a case study in how repression and TCC control came together around the health emergency. In the same month that the Indian government forced Amnesty International to close its Indian offices, the government drafted an agricultural bill that would open the floodgates to transnational agribusiness and devastate millions of farming families. Among those pushing the bill was Mukesh Ambani, CEO of the transnational conglomerate Reliance Industries, which, in 2017, turned to expanding its empire through agricultural investments. Ambani himself, the richest man in India, increased his wealth by a staggering $12 million *per hour* during the pandemic. He was not alone. The number of Indian billionaires jumped by a quarter in the first six months of the pandemic, and the combined wealth of India's richest surpassed $800 billion, a full one-third of the country's GDP and more than the combined GDP of neighboring Pakistan,

Bangladesh, Sri Lanka, Afghanistan, and Bhutan.[100] Not surprisingly, Ambani increased his wealth by strategic investments that Facebook, Google, and other tech giants made into his conglomerate (see next chapter).

The coronavirus was in many respects a blessing in disguise for the TCC and its political agents in capitalist states. It came on the heels of mass popular protests that swept six continents in fall 2019, as I will discuss in chapter three. The contagion forced protesters off the streets momentarily and gave states a respite with which to gather their repressive forces and deploy them against restive populations. The wave of repression and brutality unleashed by these states against their own citizens simply cannot be explained by the need for these states to keep them safe. To the contrary, the pandemic provided an expedient smokescreen with which to push back against the global revolt. India is again revealing. Up to 150 million workers went on strike in January 2019, the largest single labor mobilization in world history. This was followed later that year by months of protest against proposed changes to a citizenship law that would discriminate against Muslims. The curfew imposed as the pandemic hit conveniently undercut the ongoing civic uprising. When the government began to impose strict local lockdowns as the virus spread, it singled out neighborhoods identified with the protests. In these areas, heavy police barricades locked in residents for weeks.

Well before the contagion, the agents of the emerging global police state had been developing new modalities of policing and repression made possible by application of digitalization and fourth industrial revolution technologies.[101] The global police state was on full display around the world during the pandemic. Now, the post-pandemic world will see more inequality, conflict, militarism, and authoritarianism than previously, and the ruling groups will come to depend more and more on their repressive apparatuses to maintain control.

In the aftermath of the pandemic there will be new waves of mass migration to richer regions of those who lost their livelihoods and, along with it, an escalation of state repression against migrants and refugees, of racial and ethnic tensions, and of right-wing nationalism. The gravest danger is that in the face of mass struggle unleashed by the crisis the ruling classes will use the pandemic even after it has passed as a smokescreen to consolidate a global police state.[102] As I will discuss in the next chapter, the expanding global police state is fused into a new round of worldwide capitalist restructuring based on a digitalization. Early on in the pandemic former army general Stanley McChrystal recalled how "digital leadership" became crucial for the military high command of which he formed a part at the height of the US intervention in Iraq in the early 2000s. "Though units and leaders moved constantly across the battlefield, a vast majority of our interactions were by videoconference," he noted. "We became the military's ultimate remote-work force." Those "lessons of 9/11," he advised, should be applied in the post-pandemic world to the massive shift to remote work and should be embraced as permanent.[103]

GLOBAL CAPITALISM'S LEGITIMACY CRISIS

The pandemic heightened international geopolitical tensions, most spectacularly between China and the United States, as the Trump administration blamed Beijing for spreading the contagion in what was a clumsy attempt to deflect attention from its own negligence in managing the health crisis. International tensions derive from the very dynamics of global capitalism, and they will escalate dangerously in the post-pandemic world. However, an outdated nation-state/interstate mode of analysis that attributes such tensions to national rivalry and competition among national capitalist classes for international economic control is of limited utility, as I have analyzed at length elsewhere.[104] US policy toward China in recent years, including during the Trump years, sought to open China up to transnational capital—to break with continued state control over the financial system, to allow foreign investors more than a 49 percent share in corporate ownership, to remove trade restrictions, and so on. "The Chinese state has long been an important player in mediating the political and economic conditions necessary to help transform and expand global capitalism into a vast global value chain network," notes political scientist Ronald Cox with regard to US-China tensions. The battle over the extraction of surplus value from the China market, in Cox's view, is "at the center of the latest crisis of neoliberal capitalism." Competition among transnational interest blocs within the China market "has intensified under the current dynamics of global capitalist accumulation."[105] Far from a decoupling, US-China financial integration actually accelerated during the Trump years, even in 2020 in the midst of the pandemic. In that year, US-based investors held $1.1 trillion in equity issued by Chinese-based companies.[106]

Geopolitical frictions, including those surrounding US-China and US-Russia relations, are used to justify rising military budgets and stoke conflicts that open up opportunities for militarized accumulation. However, there is another fundamental dynamic at work. International tensions derive from an acute political contradiction in global capitalism: economic globalization takes place within a nation-state-based system of political authority. To put this in technical terms, there is a contradiction between the accumulation function and the legitimacy function of national states. That is, the national state faces a contradiction between the need to promote transnational capital accumulation in its territory and the need to achieve political legitimacy and stabilize the domestic social order. Attracting transnational corporate and financial investment to the national territory requires providing capital with all the incentives associated with neoliberalism, such as downward pressure on wages, deregulation, low or no taxes, privatization, investment subsidies, fiscal austerity, and on so. The result is rising inequality, impoverishment, and insecurity for working and popular classes, precisely the conditions that throw states into crises of legitimacy, destabilize national political systems, and jeopardize elite control. International frictions escalate as states, in their efforts to retain legitimacy, seek to sublimate social and political tensions and to keep the social order from fracturing. This sublimation may involve channeling social unrest toward scapegoated communities, such as immigrants in the United States (this is one key function of racism), or an external enemy, such as China or Russia, to again take the case of the United States.

The larger theoretical backdrop to this discussion is how politics, including geopolitics, may *overdetermine* economics. The state's efforts to resolve the crisis of legitimacy and stabilize the social order runs up against the accumulation strategies pursued by the TCC and capitalists' efforts in each country of the world to shift the burden of the crisis onto working and popular classes. In its attempt to secure legitimacy and assure the reproduction of the social order as a whole, the capitalist state can and often does impose restraint on capital or push the process of capital accumulation in certain directions. Yet such imposition runs up against the selfsame capitalist state's drive to promote (transnational) capital accumulation. As discussed by the French philosopher Louis Althusser, overdetermination refers to how multiple forces within a larger unity that are often contradictory or opposed to one another are active in any given political situation.[107] Most observers, fixed as they are in a state-centrism and a nation-state/interstate framework of analysis that attributes global political dynamics to capitalist competition among nation-states, fail to see how the political contradictions generated by the legitimacy crisis—in this case, the political dynamics of the pandemic—feed back into economics. For instance, in the face of the Trump administration's anti-China stance, US-based transnational corporations were hesitant to swap board seats with Chinese-based firms with which they were cross-invested. Their hesitancy was not due to intercorporate competition but because they feared that Trump's political rhetoric over China would bring them political difficulties. In this way, politics became overdetermined.[108]

On the other hand, global capitalism pits nationally constrained workers against one another and sets up the conditions for the TCC to manipulate the crises of state legitimacy and the international tensions generated by this contradiction. The problem of the relationship between capital and the state in the capitalist system is rooted in a more expansive theoretical matter, that of the relationship of the political to the economic, which I cannot take up here. Suffice it to observe that the relationship between economics and politics, between capital and political operatives and elites, is mediated in complex ways and is often tension-ridden. The capitalist state is not a mere instrument of capital, and its policies may contradict those of specific capitalist groups or of capital as a whole. The capitalist state does form a unity with capital, but we cannot collapse the two into one, just as the political and the economic are a unity that cannot be collapsed into one. Capital has the sole objective of maximizing accumulation, but capitalist states have the contradictory mandate I mentioned above.

The point is that we can expect the contradictions I am discussing here to intensify in the post-pandemic world. Splits and infighting will escalate within and among ruling groups everywhere, as they search for ways to retain legitimacy and maintain order. The drive by the capitalist state to externalize the political fallout of the crisis increases the danger that international tensions will lead to war. Historically, wars have pulled the capitalist system out of crisis, while serving to deflect attention from political tensions and problems of legitimacy. At first glance, policies and politics under crisis-ridden conditions are bewildering, unstable, and seemingly contradictory. The astute political sociologist must know how to make sense out of what may appear bewildering, to think dialectically, to see how contradictions play themselves out in unpredictable ways, to distinguish between surface appearance and underlying essence in the social phenomena we are studying. All this is important not just as an intellectual exercise, but because the more we understand our reality the better positioned we are to intervene in it.

Depending on how social and political struggles play out, structural crises like the one that began in 2008 may expand into the third type of crisis, a *systemic* crisis, meaning that the crisis must be resolved by moving beyond the existing socioeconomic system, in this case capitalism. Whether a structural crisis becomes a systemic crisis depends on a host of political and subjective factors that cannot be predicted beforehand. What is clear is that mass popular struggles against the depredations of global capitalism are now conjoined with those around the aftermath of the health emergency. While the ruling groups deploy the new technologies to enhance their control and profit-making, this same technical infrastructure of the fourth industrial revolution is producing the resources in which a political and economic system very different from the global capitalism in which we live could be achieved. If we are to free ourselves through these new technologies, however, we would first need to overthrow the oppressive and retrograde social relations of global capitalism. Let us turn to the restructuring of global capitalism now underway through a more advanced digitalization, a process that has been accelerated by the pandemic.

CHAPTER TWO

DIGITALIZED DICTATORSHIP: THE TRANSFORMATION OF GLOBAL CAPITALISM

In *The Communist Manifesto*, Karl Marx and Frederick Engels famously declared that "all that is solid melts into air" under the dizzying pace of change wrought by capitalism. Not since the Industrial Revolution of the eighteenth century has the world experienced such rapid and profound change as that ushered in by globalization. But now it appears that the system is at the brink of another round of restructuring and trans-formation based on a much more advanced digitalization of the entire global economy and society. This restructuring had already become evident in the wake of the 2008 Great Recession. But the changing social and economic conditions brought about by the coronavirus pandemic have catalyzed an acceleration of the process. These conditions have helped a new bloc of transnational capital led by the giant tech compa-nies and financial conglomerates to amass ever greater power during the pandemic and to consolidate its control over the commanding heights of the global economy. As restructuring proceeds, it will heighten the concentration of capital world-wide, worsen social inequality, and aggravate international tensions. Enabled by digital applications, the ruling groups, unless they are pushed to change course by mass pressure from below, will turn to ratcheting up the global police state to contain social upheavals.

The emerging post-pandemic capitalist paradigm is based on a digitalization and application of so-called fourth industrial revolution technologies. The new wave of technological development is made possible by a more advanced information technology. There is a growing body of literature that examines the new technologies and their varied impacts, too vast to reference here. In this chapter, I set out to build on and branch off from those works that focus on capitalist restructuring, most notably, that of Nick Srnicek, who, in 2016, published *Platform Capitalism*, an analysis of the rise to prominence of a small number of monopolistic "platform" companies such Facebook, Google, Apple, Siemens, and Uber, among others, and how they interact with the rest of the economy.[1] Led by artificial intelligence (AI) and the collection, processing, and analysis of immense amount of data ("big data"), the emerging technologies include machine learning, automation and robotics, nano- and biotechnology, the Internet of Things (IoT), quantum and cloud computing, 3D printing, virtual reality, new forms of energy storage, and autonomous vehicles, among others. Computer and information technology (CIT), first introduced in the 1980s, provided the original basis for globalization. It allowed the transnational capitalist class (TCC) to coordinate and synchronize global production sequences and, therefore, to put into place a globally integrated production and financial system into which every country has become incorporated. Just as the original introduction of CIT and the internet in the late twentieth century profoundly transformed world capitalism, this second generation of digital-based technologies is leading to a new round of worldwide restructuring that promises to have another transformative impact of the structures of the global economy, society, and polity.

THE SECOND DIGITAL AGE

Technological change is generally associated with cycles of capitalist crisis and social and political turmoil; indeed, digitalization has been spurred on by capitalist crisis. As I discussed in the previous chapter, the restructuring crisis of the 1970s led to globalization and the rise of a TCC from the 1980s onward. If "the handmill gives you a society with the feudal lord and the steam-mill gives you society with the industrial capitalist," A Sivanandan famously noted in the late twentieth century, "the microchip gives you society with the global capitalist."[2] The first generation of capitalist globalization from the 1980s onward was based on simple digitalization—the so-called third industrial revolution that was proceeded by the first such revolution, based on steam power to mechanize production, and the second, based on electrical power that led to mass production. What distinguishes the fourth from the third revolution is a fusion of the new technologies and the blurring of lines between physical, digital, and biological worlds.[3] There has been astounding progress in recent years in these new digital technologies, which are evolving at an exponential rather than linear rate. These technologies vastly enhance our physical and mental powers as a species. Their deployment in the midst of the pandemic signals an inflection point. Digitalization since its inception exhibits a network effect in so far as the gamut of human activities and social relations become plugged into the same ultimate language of streams of bits—that is, into ones and zeros. We are approaching a situation, or may well have arrived at it, in which every person on the planet is connected—for the most part directly, although everyone indirectly—through a single common digital network. Already by 2015 more than 30 percent of the global population was using social media platforms. By 2019, there were 5.2 billion smartphones in operation worldwide and more than half the planet was online.[4]

It is hard to underestimate just how rapid and extensive is the current digital restructuring of the global economy and society. According to United Nations data,[5] the "sharing economy" will surge from $14 billion in 2014 to $335 billion by 2025. Worldwide shipments of 3D printers more than doubled in 2016, to over 450,000, and were expected to reach 6.7 million by the end of 2020. The global value of e-commerce is estimated to have reached $29 trillion in 2017, which is equivalent to 36 percent of global GDP. In that year, 277 million people made cross-border purchases through e-commerce. In 2019, digitally deliverable service exports amounted to $2.9 trillion, or 50 percent of global services exports. By 2019, global internet traffic was sixty-six times the volume of the entire global internet traffic in 2005, whereas global internet protocol (IP) traffic, a proxy for data flows, grew from about 100 gigabytes (GB) *per day* in 1992 to more than 45,000 GB *per second* in 2017. Yet the world is only in the early days of the data-driven economy; by 2022, global IP traffic is projected to reach 150,700 GB per second, fueled by more and more people coming online for the first time and by the expansion of the IoT.

If the first generation of capitalist globalization from the 1980s on involved the creation of a globally integrated production and financial system, since 2008, the new wave of digitalization and the rise of platforms have facilitated a very rapid transnationalization of digital-based services. By 2017, services accounted for some 70 percent of the total gross world product and included communications, informatics, digital and platform technology, e-commerce, financial services, professional and technical work, and a host of other nontangible products, such as film and music.[6] This shift worldwide to a service-based economy based on the widespread introduction of fourth industrial technologies brings about a sea change in the structure of capitalist production toward the centrality of knowledge to the production of goods and services. This has involved the increasing dominance of intangible capital (literally, capital that is not physical in nature), what has alternatively been called "intellectual capital," "intellectual property," and "immaterial production," along with the associated concept of immaterial labor, cognitive labor, and knowledge workers, in reference to workers involved in immaterial production.

The shift has involved an ongoing reversal in the relationship of tangible to intangible capital since the late twentieth century—a reversal that accelerated in the aftermath of the 2008 Great Recession, and now in the wake of the pandemic has sped up seemingly exponentially. From an historic pattern in which tangible capital accounted for 80 percent of corporate value, by the mid-2010s intangible capital accounted for over 80 percent of value for the average corporation (we should note that financial assets, such as stocks and bonds, which derive their value from contractual claims, are considered tangible assets).[7] Graph one illustrates this reversal for the S&P 500 companies. To state this another way, intangible capital now drives material production. As the core of the global economy comes to be based on intangible capital and trade in services, the TCC—led by tech capital—has lobbied capitalist states to negotiate a new legal order and global trade regime that commodifies knowledge through copyrights, trademarks, and patents under the rubric of "intellectual property rights" and new digital trade rules. International trade negotiations began in 2013 for a Trade in Services Agreement and continued into the pandemic.[8] If earlier free trade agreements sought to bring down all barriers to the free movement of capital within and across borders, more recent negotiations have sought to remove remaining national regulations and public control of services, including finance, utilities, infrastructure, transportation, data, health, and education, in the drive to lift any barriers to trade in services (including e-commerce) and to protect intangible capital and its "intellectual property."

The coronavirus pandemic has spotlighted how essential digital services have become to the global economy. But more than shine this spotlight, the pandemic and its aftermath, to the extent that it accelerates digital restructuring, can be expected to result in a vast expansion of reduced-labor or laborless digital services, including all sorts of new telework arrangements, drone delivery, cash-free commerce, fintech

Percentage of S&P Tangible and Intangible Assets, 1975–2018

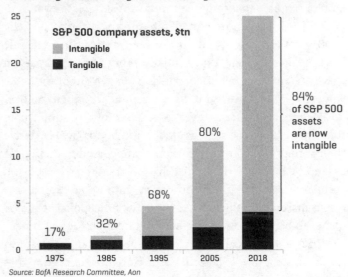

Source: BofA Research Committee, Aon

(digitalized finance), tracking and other forms of surveillance, automated medical and legal services, and remote teaching involving prerecorded instruction. The pandemic has boosted the efforts of the giant tech companies and their political agents to convert more and more areas of the economy into these new digital realms. The tech giants flourished during the contagion, as their digital services became essential to the pandemic economy, as hundreds of millions of workers worldwide moved to remote work at home or through enhanced platforms or engaged in digitally driven service work, and as in person services were replaced by remote digital services. The post-pandemic global economy now involves a more rapid and expansive application of digitalization to every aspect of global society, including war and repression.

The breakdown at the height of the pandemic of globally dispersed supply chains, so emblematic of globalization, led many to predict a wave of diversification in these supply chains, "de-globalization," and the reshoring of production and supply

chains that had previously been offshored. Globalization scholars Manfred Steger and Paul James show how the levelling
off of cross-border trade in goods and a dip in cross-border
financial flows after the 2008 crisis was more than compen-
sated for by a massive increase in global digital connection, so
that instead of deglobalization there is a shift from "embodied
globalization," by which they mean the physical mobility of
human beings, and "object-related globalization," which refers
to the mobility of physical objects, to what they term "disem-
bodied globalization," which pertains to intangible global
transactions, such as those I am here documenting.[9]

In any event, it is highly doubtful that reshoring will
somehow bring back to rich countries stable, high-skilled, and
high-paying industrial and postindustrial jobs, given that the
relocation back to the core centers of the global economy will
involve high levels of automation, as I discuss below. (As a
side note, reshoring, or "de-globalization," does not mean that
capital ceases to be transnational.[10] It is *transnational capital*
that relocates from one place to another as the geography of
global capitalism is continuously reconfigured). The flip side
of reshoring to rich counties is the automation of plants that
were offshored. Sweatshops that largely employ young women
in cheap labor zones around the world, perhaps the archetypi-
cal image of the global economy, may become rarer, as the
low-skilled and repetitive labor that these sweatshops employ
are exactly the type of tasks that are easily automated. As early
as 2012, following a wave of strikes that year by its workers
in China, Foxcomm, the Taiwanese-based conglomerate that
assembles iPads and other electronic devices, announced
that it would replace one million workers with robots. In fact,
official Chinese statistics report a decline of thirty million
manufacturing jobs from 1996 to 2014, 25 percent of the total,
even as manufacturing output increased by over 70 percent.[11]

On the other hand, digitalization drives the expansion
of cross-border services, as electronic offshoring, unlike the

overseas relocation of production facilities, is virtually frictionless and does not add transportation and other ancillary costs, such as customs charges. By 2016, the production of CIT goods and services represented 6.5 percent of global GDP and one hundred million people were employed in the CIT service sector.[12] When work is carried out remotely, it does not matter where it is performed. The surge in investment in remote working during the pandemic opens the door to increased trade in digital services. Yet even for services, new digital technologies, such as interactive voice response systems, are reducing the requirement for direct person-to-person communication and may lead to the automation of call centers around the world. In the coming years, we may see a mix of reshoring to rich countries and increased automation in areas that became labor-intensive industrial processing zones and service centers, such as China's Guangdong Province. In the long run, it may be that offshoring is a historical way station on the road to automation.

Anecdotes from around the world on new waves of digitalization and automation are as fascinating as they are frightening. In Japan, seven-foot robots that stack convenience store shelves have been introduced in the midst of the pandemic to two popular store franchises, FamilyMart and Lawson. Unlike earlier retail robots introduced in the United States by Walmart to scan shelf inventory or by warehouses in which the robots pick up and deposit the same things from the same place in repetitive operations, the Japanese robots can grasp different shapes and sizes and place them into different locations as they move about the store. The robots are controlled by a "human pilot" operating in virtual reality, who is not present in the store, can operate multiple robots, and may, in fact, physically be anywhere on the planet. According to one spokesperson for Telexistence, the Japanese startup that developed the robot, workers who control the robots can be hired from overseas in places that offer lower labor costs.[13]

Evolution of Global Market of Internet of Things (in $ billions)

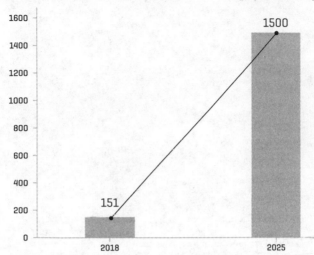

Source: United Nations Conference on Trade and Development (UNCTAD). Digital economy report 2019: value creation and capture, implications for developing countries, 2019, p.9

As impressive as the take-off of the new round of digitalization appears, this second digital age, to reiterate, is still in its infancy. For instance, blockchain technologies, or "distributed ledger technologies," that allow multiple parties to engage in secure transactions without any intermediaries, including financial transactions, had barely gotten off the ground by 2020. Blockchain first became known in the 2010s as the technology that made cryptocurrencies, such as Bitcoin, possible and will constitute the technological infrastructure for a more general shift to digital money in the future (as the use of digital currency spreads, it will bring us closer to dethroning the domination of the dollar, but that is a story for elsewhere). In fact, blockchain business value is expected to explode toward the end of the 2020s, reaching an estimated $3 trillion by the end of the decade.[14] The truly momentous effects of big data are yet to be felt. Big data exploded onto the scene in the early twenty-first century. In 2000, only one-quarter of the world's stored information was digitalized, but by 2013 only 2 percent

Global Internet Protocol Traffic (in Gb per second)

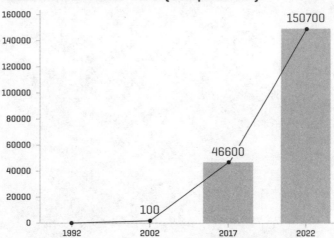

Source: United Nations Conference on Trade and Development (UNCTAD), Digital economy report 2019: value creation and capture, implications for developing countries, 2019, p.9

of all stored information was nondigital. One 2017 IBM report noted that 2.5 quadrillion bytes of data were created every day in that year, and that "90 percent of the data in the world today has been created in the last two years alone."[15]

Much of fourth industrial revolution technology central to the digital restructuring of global capitalism is dependent for its widespread introduction on 5G (fifth generation broadband technology), which first began rolling out in 2019 and can be considered the essential underlying infrastructure (along with cloud computing) for the second digital age. Rolled out in the 1980s, the first commercial automated cellular network, 1G, enabled voice calls between mobile technologies. This analog technology was replaced by the digitalized 2G network in the 1990s, which made text messaging possible. In the 2000s, 3G opened up the transmission of data and made smartphones possible. In the following decade, 4G further optimized data transmission and enabled streaming video. Now, the greater bandwidth of 5G makes possible higher download speeds (up to 10 gigabits per second) that are required for the emerging digital technologies, in particular, the IoT (machine to machine connections), blockchain, and the much more rapid and extensive collection and processing of data. Closely correlated with 5G technology is cloud computing necessary to store and process the vast new quantities of data, including for a wide range of e-commerce and applications that allow for remote work. Cloud computing experienced a rapid expansion during the pandemic, accounting for 10 percent of all technology spending and attracted tens of billions of dollars in corporate investment.[16]

THE NEW CAPITAL BLOC

The era of globalization has involved an ongoing radical transformation in the modalities of producing and appropriating surplus value, a transformation hastened first by the 2008 crisis and now again by the pandemic. At the center of global restructuring are the giant tech companies, among them Microsoft, Apple, Amazon, Tencent, Alibaba, and Facebook. These companies experienced astonishing growth in the 2010s. Added now to the earlier tech behemoths are Zoom, Netflix, and other companies boosted by the pandemic, as well as tech firms like Taiwan Semiconductor Manufacturing (TSM), whose expansion and market capitalization was ballooning even before the contagion. Zoom daily users jumped by 3000 percent in the first four months of the pandemic.[17] In 2020, Apple and Microsoft registered an astounding market capitalization of $1.4 trillion each in early 2020, on the eve of the pandemic. By the end of that year, this figure had jumped to $2.08 trillion and $1.63 trillion, respectively. Amazon's capitalization stood at $1.04 trillion going into the pandemic and had climbed to $1.58 trillion by the end of 2020. Alphabet (Google's parent company) registered a $1.2 trillion capitalization, Samsung $983 billion, Facebook $779 billion, and Alibaba and Tencent some $700 billion each.[18] To give an idea of just how rapidly these tech behemoths have grown, Google's market capitalization went from under $200 billion in 2008 to over one $1 trillion in 2020, or a 500 percent increase over the decade.[19] Meanwhile, in just two years, from 2015 to 2017, the combined value of the platform companies with a market capitalization of more than $100 million jumped by 67 percent, to more than $7 trillion.[20] It must be stressed that both the pace of change and the magnitude of global capital is simply without precedent, so that these figures and others identified in this book are bound to be outdated even before this study reaches my readers.

The cluster of giant tech firms that generate, extract, and process data have absorbed enormous amounts of cash from transnational investors from around the world who, desperate for new investment opportunities, have poured billions of dollars into the tech and platform companies as an outlet for their surplus accumulated capital. Annual investment in CIT jumped from $17 billion in 1970 to $65 billion in 1980, then to $175 billion in 1990, $496 billion in 2000, and $654 billion in 2016, topped $800 billion in 2019, and then predictably spiked again during the pandemic, approaching $1 trillion by the end of 2020.[21] As capitalists invest these billions, the global banking and investment houses become interwoven with tech capital, as do businesses across the globe that are moving to cloud computing and artificial intelligence. Moreover, the tech giants are purchasing bonds floated by transnational corporations in other sectors of the global economy as a way to hedge their enormous financial assets across a range of investments.[22] By the second decade of the century, the global economy came to be characterized above all by the twin processes of digitalization and financialization.

Data shows that from the 1980s onward, those corporations that transitioned to CIT were dramatically more productive than their competitors, managing to resolve the so-called "productivity paradox," whereby the growth in productivity notably slowed starting in 1973, the date of the onset of a structural crisis and subsequent globalization.[23] As a result the center of gravity in the circuits of accumulation began to shift toward those corporations developing and producing CIT. Digitalization is a "general purpose technology," meaning that, like electricity, it spreads throughout all branches of the economy and society and becomes built into everything. Those who control the development and application of digital technologies acquire newfound social power and political influence. As this process deepens, those TCC groups that control general digitalization develop new modalities for organizing the extraction of relative surplus value and increasing productivity at an exponential rate. Hence, the new technologies disrupt existing value chains and generate a reorganization among sectors of capital and fractions of the capitalist class. They allow the tech giants and digitalized finance capital to appropriate ever-greater shares of the value generated by global circuits of accumulation.

In this process there emerge new configurations and blocs of capital. The rise of the digital economy involves a fusion of Silicon Valley with transnational finance capital—US bank investment in tech, for instance, increased by 180 percent from 2017 to 2019[24]—and the military-industrial-security complex, giving rise to a new bloc of capital that appears to be at the very core of the emerging post-pandemic paradigm. This new bloc is emerging even more powerful than it was going into the health emergency, spurring a vast new centralization and concentration of capital on a global scale. At the head of this bloc, the tech behemoths are larger financial entities than most countries in the world and are able to wield enormous influence over capitalist states. New York state governor Mario Cuomo showcased this emerging capital-state relation in early May 2020, when he appointed three tech billionaires, Eric Schmidt of Google, Apple, and Facebook, former Microsoft CEO Bill Gates, and Michael Bloomberg, to head up a Blue Ribbon Commission to come up with plans to outsource public schools, hospitals, policing, and other public services to private tech companies.[25] Such "public-private partnerships" privatize to capital traditional state functions, while converting public funds into corporate subsidies.

While it is true that US- and Chinese-based corporations dominate the global tech sector, I have shown in my earlier research, and more recently sociologist Peter Phillips has documented in his study *Giants: The Global Power Elite*,[26] how transnational capital has become so interpenetrated that there are no major concentrations of capital outside of the interconnected mass. Moreover, there are now hundreds of up-and-coming tech firms from around the world that have prospered during the pandemic and can be expected to expand rapidly as restructuring proceeds. Rather than referring to nations, by the *new bloc* I am alluding to the cutting edge of accumulation that is what is most at the inner core of global circuits of accumulation central to the very generation of value. As digitalization disrupts previously established value chains, these new clusters and branches of capital become amalgamated, and as these new clusters and branches of capital become amalgamated, this shift toward the new bloc is captured by the notion of *center of gravity*. While the contours of this new bloc were already in focus before the pandemic, the contagion accelerated the shift in the leading edge of accumulation. Entire industries, from airlines, leisure and hotel, mall-based retail establishments, and entertainment companies, such as movie theaters, were forced to downsize and even suspend operations during the pandemic, while simultaneously the opportunities for the emerging bloc of capital expanded dramatically.

Emblematic of the sudden windfall to tech capital afforded by the pandemic and of how the new bloc is becoming the center of gravity of global accumulation is the case of Draganfly corporation, a Canadian-based manufacturer of military and civilian drones. According to one 2020 report:

Like the rest of the world, Canadian drone maker Draganfly has been anxiously watching the spread of the novel coronavirus. And when COVID-19 cases started springing up across Washington nursing homes in mid-February, the team began brainstorming. By March, Draganfly had licensed the machine vision and AI tech needed to offer social distancing and health monitoring services from the air. Demand to test the technology was 'insatiable,' not just from government and law enforcement, but also from health care, airline, cruise, hospitality, theme park, and other commercial industries. By mid-April, the police department in Westport, Connecticut had a pilot underway, the first of its kind in the U.S. [Company spokesperson] Chell says Draganfly has been 'inundated' with requests from other jurisdictions, while the numbers on the private side 'are even more prolific. As federal and local governments wrestle with the coronavirus pandemic—from tracking the spread of COVID-19 to gauging when to lift restrictions—everyone is taking a closer look at autonomous technologies like drones and robots.[27]

Similarly, in conjunction with the tech sector, the pandemic presented the global medical and pharmaceutical industry with numerous potential windfalls. It is predicted that global digital health revenue from various forms of telemedicine and related services will rise from $350 billion in 2019 to over $600 billion in 2024, as the global multitrillion-dollar health care market becomes restructured through digitalization. Billions in equity funding flowed into private digital health corporations as equity investment doubled during 2020 alone.[28] Propelled forward by digitalization, biotechnology stands at the cutting edge of the fourth industrial revolution. Developments in biotechnology and bioengineering came together "with a host of complex sensory mechanisms to bring about a significant shift in the life sciences," notes Timothy Erik Strom. He continues: "Building on the constitutive forces that enabled the origin of cybernetic capitalism in the military-industrial complex of the Second World War, the rise of biotech brought a tighter weave to the alliance between state-induced research, corporate power over technology, and finance capital, with the combination radically altering humanity's relationship with the natural world."[29]

In 2010, Craig Venter, the CEO of the biotech company Celera Genomics announced that he had created "the first self-replicating species on the planet whose parent is a computer." For first time ever, he explained, a private biotech company assembled out of computer information real DNA that was then used to create a new virus—that is, to create a new life form out of inorganic material. Venter defined the technology as "synthetic genomics." It would "start in the computer in the digital world from digitized biology and make new DNA constructs for very specific purposes," that is, for commercial purposes.[30] Synthetic genomics, in turn, has been combined with another area of biotechnology, "gain of function" research, which as I discussed in the previous chapter, starts with an already existing life form and modifies its structure. The pharmaceutical industry stands to cash in massively on diseases and new therapies made possible through such biotechnology breakthroughs. Early in the pandemic, Gilead Sciences, a biotech/pharmaceutical company, developed a prototype drug, Remdesivir, as a therapeutic aid (not a vaccine) for treating Covid-19 patients. The drug gained notoriety after it was used to treat US president Donald Trump when he caught the virus in October 2020. The company's stock price surged after the WHO commended the experimental drug early on in the pandemic.[31]

In the absurdly perverse world of capitalism, everything that occurs in society, including vaccines against Covid-19 and other biotechnology breakthroughs, must be subjected to the logic of capital accumulation. So long as this is the case, humanity will be simply unable to benefit from the enormous opportunities opened up by new biotechnologies. Cancer, hepatitis C, heart disease, and a host of other deadly ailments are banes for hundreds of millions of people. Yet the treatment of these diseases constitutes a multitrillion-dollar industry, immensely profitable for pharmaceutical companies, private hospitals, and manufacturers of medical equipment, among others. Preventative medicine is simply not profitable. The treasure chest to capital lies in treatments that simply slow the decline in the health of patients or ameliorate symptoms without eliminating the underlying causes of pathologies or in creating additional patients so as to convert them into life-time customers. There are now antiretroviral drugs that treat people for the symptoms of HIV, yet the virus continues to spread throughout the world, as do such diseases as malaria and tuberculosis, even as the global cosmetic surgery market is expected to surpass $40 billion by 2025,[32] and each year US citizens spend tens of millions of dollars on plastic surgery for their pets.[33] Revolutionary breakthroughs in health care are only available to the rich through the prism of medicine for profit. New medical technologies are now capable of restoring hearing to the deaf, sight to the blind, and providing robotic limbs to quadriplegics, but the majority are locked out of these medical miracles.

Goldman Sachs, one of the biggest investment houses in the world, displayed this impeccable logic of capital, warning in 2018 report that gene therapies that cure diseases were bad for business. The report referenced Gilead Sciences, the biotech/pharmaceutical company that developed a treatment for hepatitis C, which achieved cure rates of more than 90 percent. The company's US sales for the treatment, observed the report, peaked at $12.5 billion in 2015, but then steadily fell:

> Is curing patients a sustainable business model? The potential to deliver 'one shot cures' is one of the most

attractive aspects of gene therapy, genetically-engineered cell therapy and gene editing. However, such treatments offer a very different outlook with regard to recurring revenue versus chronic therapies. While the proposition offers tremendous value for patients and society, it could represent a challenge for genome medicine developers looking for sustained cash flows.... [Gilead Sciences] is a case in point, where the success of its hepatitis C franchise has gradually exhausted the available pool of treatable patients. In the case of infectious diseases such as hepatitis C, curing existing patients also decreases the number of carriers able to transmit the virus to new patients, thus the incident pool also declines.... Where an incident pool remains stable (e.g., in cancer) the potential for a cure poses less risk to the sustainability of a franchise.[34]

The digital restructuring of global capitalism is driven by big data, which exploded onto the scene in the early twenty-first century. As mentioned above, in 2000, only one-quarter of the world's stored information was digitalized, but, by 2013, only 2 percent of all stored information was nondigital. One 2017 IBM report noted that 2.5 quadrillion bytes of data were created every day in that year, and that "90 percent of the data in the world today has been created in the last two years alone."[35] This "datafication" was not merely in terms of size but also in the ability to quantify aspects of the world not previously quantified, such as location information captured, amassed, and processed through GPS satellite systems. Previously, information was chiefly captured through sampling as a statistical method first introduced in the late nineteenth century that involved a random sample followed by inference to the population universe. But, now, as Cukier and Mayer-Schoenberger observe, big data involves collecting *all* the data of the entire population in concern, that is, we are shifting from sampling data to "data-n," to use the terminology of statistics.[36] Data is becoming an immensely valuable asset and the lifeblood of the digital economy. The firms that control big data are able to exercise decisive influence over the economy as a whole, including feeding into machines (artificial intelligence) the data necessary for the algorithms that drive production and commerce. As this process deepens, algorithms increasingly organize the circuits of capital accumulation.

In her study *The Age of Surveillance Capitalism*, Shoshona Zuboff of the Harvard Business School shows how data extraction and analysis has reached a height of ubiquity unimaginable only a few years ago. But her liberal analysis is concerned with how "raw surveillance capitalism" supposedly distorts the competitive market—that surveillance through data is a rogue form that has undermined a happier era of "democratic capitalism" and "market democracy." Unregulated data, in her view, is "a threat to capitalism itself" that can be addressed by regulation. But advanced digitalization and surveillance through big data is not some rupture with an earlier capitalism. As we have seen, far from an aberration, it springs from the "normal" dynamics of capital accumulation and contradictions internal to capitalist development.[37] Moreover, along with new opportunities for corporate profit-making, big data immensely enhances the social control powers of both states and capital beyond surveillance alone. French philosopher Michel Foucault had pointed out in many of his works that preceded the digital age how states and "disciplinary regimes" create and use data to exercise control over populations. Political scientist James Scott, in his study *Seeing Like a State*, identified how states' drive to collect data and quantify everything leads to heightened state control over communities.[38] Both Foucault and Scott were writing before the age of big data, which now makes possible a more all-pervasive Big Brother—an expanding global police state—epitomized in so-called "predictive policing," in which populations are criminalized in the absence of the actual commission of a crime.[39]

Cukier and Mayer-Schoenberger observe (not unapprovingly, I should note) how big data allowed for a dramatic increase in the vacate orders issued to poor people by the New York City government during the mayoralty of Michael Bloomberg, whose multibillion-dollar fortune was made in the data business. This was done through the creation of a database of every one of the 900,000 buildings in the city, involving the amalgamation of data from nineteen city agencies on tax liens, anomalies in utility usage, service cuts, missed payments, local crime rates, rodent complaints, and more. The amassing, merging, and processing of all this data allowed building inspectors to increase the number of vacate orders they issued following an inspection from 13 percent of building visits to 70 percent.[40] This in the midst of an acute housing crisis in New York and other big US cities that has led many poor families to share apartments lest they live in the streets. In my own city, Los Angeles, in 2020, there were at least 134,000 people living in the streets on any given day, and in the first ten months of that year nearly 1,000 homeless people died, even as 93,000 housing units sat vacant because would-be tenants could not afford the rent.[41] The larger story here is how big data and digitalization is transforming welfare systems worldwide, in what one report termed "automating poverty," including the fact that millions of citizens who lack digital skills or access are being barred from accessing their welfare and social service rights.[42]

The second leg in the new triangulated bloc is transnational finance capital. Money capital is the universal and most mobile form of capital and also the most globalized. Money (value) moves seamlessly and instantaneously across the globe through the digitalized global financial system that predated by several decades the current restructuring. But finance is also undergoing a revolution driven by digital restructuring, as competition heats up for shares of the $1.5 trillion global pool of financial industry profits. Digital payment platforms are rapidly replacing earlier forms of payment. In the United States, payments through the US network Venmo increased by 52 percent during the pandemic, while in Latin America payments through the Mercado Pago network rose by 14.12 percent. In 2020, conventional banks accounted for only 72 percent of the stock market value of the global banking and payments industry, down from 81 percent at the start of the pandemic, and 96 percent in 2010. As financialization deepens, transnational capital, octopus-like, has extended its tentacles into every branch and sector of the global economy. BlackRock is emblematic of how it has become interwoven in particular with tech and the military-industrial complex. With some $8 trillion in assets under its management in 2020, BlackRock was already, pre-pandemic, one of the largest shareholders in the leading transnational corporations, owning multibillion-dollar stakes in the tech and military-industrial giants, as well as in energy, pharmaceutical, retail, media, and entertainment complexes. On the eve of the pandemic, BlackRock CEO Larry Fink predicted, "In the near future, and sooner than most expect, there will be a significant reallocation of capital."[43]

Bank of America, one of the largest global banking conglomerates, conducted a survey of three thousand of the largest companies in twenty-five economic sectors. Among these sectors, the report identified "enablers for the world—post-Covid," including health care, technology, digital, consumer staples, industrial real estate, and ESG. This latter is an acronym for Environmental, Social, and Governance, which includes the development of the IoT, telecom infrastructure, and security. The report predicted a rise in IT spending and an escalation of corporate tech wars, some of it expressed in geopolitics, led by a wave of investment in infrastructure, AI technologies, and moonshot future tech. The phrase "moon-shot future tech" was coined by Google in reference to venture investments in new "groundbreaking" technologies that do not necessarily register immediate profitability, such as autonomous vehicles, quantum computing, and vertical farming. Half of the corporations surveyed said they expected to increase technology investments in the wake of the pandemic, and 44 percent specified that the increase would be in robots and automation. The report further broke down winners and losers. Leading the winners, unsurprisingly, were tech service providers, new media and entertainment, big tech platforms, tech hardware, e-commerce, payments and "other diversified financial wealth," data centers, biopharma and biotech, food and household staples, life sciences and "tools-diagnostics," med-tech and health tech, capital goods and industrial automation, defense, software, semiconductors, cloud and software services, integrated utilities, and renewable utility grids. Some of the losers were, predictably, "old" media and entertainment, autos, general and apparel retail, travel and leisure, oil and gas, banks (this distinct from new forms of finance capital such as investment houses, fund management, and so on), offices, commercial shopping, malls, and lodging.[44]

Throughout the world, we are seeing a novel fusion of tech and finance capital around nontraditional forms of digital finance. In Latin America, digital bank and e-commerce pioneers such as Nubank and MercadoLibre (owner of Mercado Pago) are capturing major shares of industry. In Southeast Asia, the ride-hailing service companies Asia Grab and Gojek introduced apps that also turned them into financial firms. In 2020, such fintech firms provided the majority of consumer loans in Sweden. In the United States, credit card firms, such as Visa, digital finance giants, such as PayPal, and conventional banks compete for financial market shares. Tech giants, such as Alibaba, Apple, and Alphabet, are establishing fintech branches.[45] Alibaba manages the most integrated fintech platform in the world—ANT—which, in 2019, handled a whopping $16 trillion in payments and operations, ranging from loans to digital credit card services, investment, and insurance brokerage—in the words of the *Economist*, "the world's purest example of the tremendous potential of digital finance."[46]

The new bloc of capital is able to appropriate through digitalization and the circuits of distribution greater portions of surplus value generated elsewhere in the global economy, especially as value flows through a porous financial system. "In the new business models of the digital economy, two emerging and related forces are increasingly driving value creation: platformization and the monetization of the rapidly expanding volume of digital data," noted the United Nations Conference on Trade and Development (UNCTAD) in a report issued in the midst of the pandemic. "Digital platforms are central actors in this economy, and digital data have become a key resource in economic processes, which can lead to value creation."[47] The critical point, however, is not so much that tech capital, in its fusion with the financial industry, necessarily creates this value; rather, its inordinate control over the digitalization process means that it can *appropriate* value created throughout the global economy. Data in and of itself cannot create value; only labor can. Data may work to enhance the production of surplus value (and then appropriate it from other capitals that directly extract that surplus value) or it may appropriate that value through such channels as advertising revenue. In this way, big data is turned into big profit for capitals that control such data. The UNCTAD noted:

> In the traditional economy, property rights in well-established markets comprising producers and consumers strongly determine who is the beneficiary of the value of the corresponding goods and services. With regard to data, the situation is less clear, as it is difficult to establish "ownership" of the data. Indeed, given the specific characteristics of data, ownership may not even

be the appropriate term. The value of personal data is tied to the data subject or producer, and this cannot be sold. What matters more are the control, access and rights over the data. Under the current system (or non-system), digital platforms are often the main collectors or extractors of data and can therefore appropriate the value. The data sources (i.e. the data producers or data subjects) are not able to capture any part of the economic value created with their data.[48]

The third leg in this triangulated bloc of capital is the military-industrial-security complex. As the tech industry emerged in the 1990s, it was conjoined at birth to the military-industrial-security complex and the global police state.[49] Over the years, for instance, Google has supplied mapping technology used by the US Army in Iraq, hosted data for the Central Intelligence Agency, indexed the National Security Agency's vast intelligence databases, built military robots, co-launched a spy satellite with the Pentagon, and leased its cloud computing platform to help police departments predict crime. The other tech giants are similarly intertwined with the military-industrial-security complex.[50] The marriage between the tech industry and the US intelligence and covert operations complex became further cemented in the midst of the pandemic, when the Central Intelligence Agency announced that it had awarded its Commercial Cloud Enterprise (known as C2E), potentially worth "tens of billions" of dollars (the exact amounts remains undisclosed), on behalf of seventeen intelligence agencies to five companies—Amazon, Microsoft, Google, Oracle, and IBM.[51]

The rise of the digital economy blurs the boundaries between military and civilian sectors of the economy and between the state and corporations, as it brings together finance, the military-industrial complex, and tech companies around a combined process of financial speculation and militarized accumulation. The concepts of *militarized accumulation* and, relatedly, *accumulation by repression,* as I have developed them in my 2020 study *The Global Police State* help us identify how transnational capital has become more and more dependent on a global war economy that in turn relies on perpetual state organized war-making, social control, and repression and is driven by the new digital technologies. Worldwide, total defense outlays grew by 50 percent from 2006 to 2015, from $1.4 trillion to $2.03 trillion, although this figure does not take into account secret budgets, contingency operations, and "homeland security" spending. During this time, military-industrial complex profits quadrupled. By 2018, private military companies employed some fifteen million people around the world, while another twenty million people worked in private security.

The new systems of warfare, social control, and repression are driven by digital technology. The market for new social control systems made possible by digital technology runs into the hundreds of billions of dollars. The global biometrics market, for instance, was expected to jump from its $15 billion value in 2015 to $35 billion by 2020.[52] The new technologies of social control span artificial intelligence–powered autonomous weaponry, such as unmanned attack and transportation vehicles, robot soldiers, a new generation of superdrones and flybots, hypersonic weapons, microwave guns that immobilize, cyberattack and info-warfare, biometric identification, state data mining, and global electronic surveillance that allows for the tracking and controlling of every movement. State and corporate surveillance are melding into a single omnipresent system. The surveillance powers applied for the pandemic became normalized and repurposed for heightened political control and corporate dominance through the emerging state-corporate surveillance complex. The pandemic, as we saw in the previous chapter, aggravated all of the social and political contradictions of a global capitalism in deep crisis. It became even more politically necessary than prior to the outbreak for the ruling groups to wield the global police state to contain discontent from below at the same time as the pandemic itself presented the TCC with new opportunities for militarized accumulation and accumulation by repression.

LABOR AND CAPITAL IN THE SECOND DIGITAL AGE

"The role of humans as the most important factor of
production is bound to diminish in the same way that
the role of horses in agricultural production was first
diminished and then eliminated by the introduction
of the tractor."
—Wassily Leontief, Nobel laureate in economics, 1983[53]

The capitalist system is by its nature expansionary. Just as riding a bicycle, in which the bike collapses if one stops pedaling, capitalism collapses if it stops expanding. World capitalism has gone through ongoing cycles of crisis followed by waves of expansion. In each earlier structural crisis, the system went through a new round of extensive expansion, that is, incorporation of new territories and populations—from waves of colonial conquest in earlier centuries to the integration in the late twentieth and early twenty-first centuries of the former socialist bloc countries, China, India, and other areas that had been marginally outside the system. There are very few pockets of territories and peoples, if any, around the world that have yet to be incorporated through this process of *extensive* (outward) expansion. What is left for global capital, increasingly, is *intensive* expansion, involving the commodification of what were noncommodified resources and activities. Commodification refers to the process of turning people, the things that people produce, and nature into things that are privately owned, have a monetary value, and can be bought and sold. The juggernaut of commodification now targets the accelerated privatization of health and educational systems, infrastructure, and other public services, public lands, and nature reserves, and even military and police forces.

But this commodification involves a double movement. First, transnational capital seeks to open up new opportunities for accumulation by seizing what remains outside its domain and turning it into assets, in particular, an ever more violent appropriation of nature and the public domain. Second and closely related, transnational capital seeks to sustain the rate of profit by replacing workers with technology and by pushing down wages and other labor costs through deskilling and fragmentation of the labor process. It seeks in this effort to transfer the cost of reproducing labor from the wage—what capitalists have to pay to workers for them to reproduce their existence—to states precisely at a time when state services are themselves being gutted and privatized. Marx theorized that the cost of labor power (the wage) is the cost for the reproduction of labor power, that is, the cost of the workers' social reproduction. If the price of labor power dipped below this minimum, workers could not survive long enough to return to work to produce more surplus value (profit). He wrote:

> Wages will rise and fall according to the relation of supply and demand, according to the turn taken by the competition between the buyers of labor power, the capitalists, and the sellers of labor power, the workers. The fluctuations in wages correspond in general to the fluctuations in prices of commodities. Within these fluctuations, however, the price of labor power will be determined by the cost of production, by the labor time necessary to produce this commodity—labor power. What, then, is the cost of production of labor power? It is the cost required for maintaining the worker as a worker and of developing him into a worker.

To the extent that capital is more and more transnational (outside of home territory), combined with the expansion of the ranks of surplus labor worldwide, global capital as a totality can more and more dispense with the social wage. To put this in simplified terms, the more capital can freely move around the globe and the more there is a mass of humanity that is unemployed and marginalized, the less the capitalist class needs to worry about paying wages with which those they employ can survive. This survival is what we may call social reproduction. Social reproduction becomes ever more externalized, forced onto households and communities. In other words, the price of labor can dip below the cost of the reproduction of labor so long as this externalization of social reproduction holds. David Harvey has long observed that capitalists in the geographic centers of the world capitalist system have been able to overcome waves of crises by displacing these crises in time and space as temporary "fixes"—shifting these crises onto more vulnerable regions or postponing them further into the future without having to reckon with them.[54] But at a certain point the system may no longer have anywhere to spatially displace crises or the ability to displace them temporally, which heightens the pressures for a reduction of the total global wage bill—that is, pressures build up for capitalists to unload the crisis on the backs of workers or to quicken the process of replacing workers with technology. Marx continues:

> The price of the cost of existence and reproduction constitutes wages. Wages so determined are called the *wage minimum*. This wage minimum, like the determination of the price of commodities by the cost of production in general, does not hold good for the *single individual* but for the *species*. Individual workers, millions of workers, do not get enough to be able to exist and reproduce themselves; but the wages of the whole working class level down, within their fluctuations, to this minimum.[55]

This process described by the ever-prescient Marx is driven forward by the new wave of digitalization, accelerated now in hothouse fashion by the economic and social conditions thrown up by the pandemic. Crises, let us recall, provide transnational capital with the opportunity to restore profit levels by forcing greater productivity out of fewer workers. Since the 1980s, almost all employment lost in the United States in routine occupations due to automation, for instance, occurred during recessions.[56] The first wave of CIT in the latter decades of the twentieth century triggered explosive growth in productivity and productive capacities, while the new digital technologies promise to multiply such capacities many times over. Specifically, digitalization vastly increases what radical political economists, following Marx, refer to as the organic composition of capital, meaning that the portion of fixed capital in the form of machinery and technology tends to increase relative to variable capital in the form of labor. In laymen's terms, digitalization greatly accelerates the process whereby machinery and technology replace human labor, thus expanding the ranks of those who are made surplus and marginalized.

This process described by Marx is evident today. One US National Bureau of Economic Research report found that each new robot introduced in a locale results in a loss of 3 to 5.6 jobs.[57] In 1990, the top three carmakers in Detroit had a market capitalization of $36 billion and 1.2 million employees. In 2014, the top three firms in Silicon Valley, with a market capitalization of over $1 trillion had only 137,000 employees.[58] As Brynjolfsson and McAfee recount, a team of just fifteen people created a single app, Instagram, that, shortly after it was launched, had over 130 million customers who shared billions of photos. Within fifteen months of its founding in 2010, the company was sold to Facebook, which in turn reached one billion users in 2012, although it employed only 4,600 people. In contrast, they note, Kodak, a giant in photographic technology prior to the digital age, also helped customers share billions of photos over the decades, yet it directly employed 145,300 people and indirectly employed thousands more through the vast supply chain of retail redistribution that is now made redundant by digital distribution.[59] In a fatal twist of irony, Instagram was sold just months after Kodak declared bankruptcy.

The increase in the organic composition of capital may bring profit windfalls to certain sectors of capital, yet it also aggravates overaccumulation and social polarization. Expanded inequalities, as we saw in the previous chapter, have reached unprecedented levels worldwide. They end up undermining the stability of the system as the gap grows between what is (or could be) produced and what the market can absorb. The extreme concentration of the planet's wealth in the hands of the few and the accelerated impoverishment and dispossession of the majority means that transnational capital had increasing difficulty in finding productive outlets to unload enormous amounts of surplus it accumulated. As I noted earlier, the total cash held in reserves of the world's two thousand biggest nonfinancial corporations increased from $6.6 trillion in 2010 to $14.2 trillion in 2020, even as the global economy stagnated.[60] But capital cannot remain idle indefinitely without ceasing to be capital. Beyond financial speculation, printing more money, debt-driven growth, and investment in the global police state, the TCC—or at least its organic intellectuals—is hedging its bets on the current wave of restructuring opening up enough new opportunities for investing overaccumulated capital in the new technologies and circuits of accumulation.

It is certainly possible that restructuring will unleash a new wave of expansion, but any such expansion will run up against the problems discussed previously that an increase in the organic composition of capital presents for the system, namely, the tendency for the rate of profit to fall and the amassing of profits that cannot be profitably reinvested. With heightened digitalization brought about by the pandemic there will be tens, even hundreds, of millions who lost their jobs and will not be reabsorbed into the labor force as technology takes over their former tasks. One University of Chicago study estimated that 42 percent of pandemic layoffs in the United States would result in permanent job loss.[61] As well, large corporations will snatch up millions of small businesses forced into bankruptcy—the ILO estimates that some 436 million such businesses are at risk worldwide and may be snatched up by the giant combines and investment houses, thus heightening the concentration of capital worldwide.[62] Several US government research reports found that the pandemic accelerated the pace of automation and exacerbated automation's impact on job loss.[63] "Even after the pandemic, the threat of future pandemics and the massive technological transition into the virtual world induced by the pandemic could induce significant shifts in the labor market and provide a catalyst for more automation in the long run," observed a Federal Reserve Bank study. "Recent technological developments have made more previously safe jobs automatable... forc[ing] an experiment of various technologies and innovations that was unprecedented in its scale and scope."[64]

Many mainstream accounts put forward a fairy-tale version of the fourth industrial revolution as ushering in a new age of democracy, prosperity, and abundance for all. This *potential* is subverted by capitalism, in so far as the technologies are applied by capital and its political agents to enhance social control and intensify the extraction of surplus value (profits), and amass private wealth, as brought home by the pandemic.[65] With regard to the world of work, for many years, the apologists of global capitalism have claimed that the digital economy will bring high-skilled, high-paid jobs and resolve problems of social polarization and stagnation. It is true that the first wave of digitalization in the late twentieth century resulted in a bifurcation of work, generating high-paid, high-skilled jobs on one side of the pole, giving rise to new armies of tech and finance workers, engineers, software programmers, and so on. On the other side of the pole, digitalization produced a much more numerous mass of deskilled, low-wage workers and an expansion of the ranks of surplus labor. But the new wave of digitalization now threatens to make redundant much so-called "knowledge work" and to deskill and downgrade a significant portion of those knowledge-based jobs that remain. Increasingly, cognitive labor and gig workers face low wages, dull repetitive tasks, and precariousness. As "big data" captures data on knowledge-based occupations at the workplace and in the market, and then converts it into algorithms, this labor itself is threatened with replacement by artificial intelligence, autonomous vehicles, and the other fourth industrial revolution technologies. Algorithms are built into all aspects of the labor process and come to underpin the organization of capitalist exploitation. Digitally driven production ultimately seeks to achieve what the Nike Corporation refers to as "engineering the labor out of the product."[66]

The transformations that CIT promises to bring are distinct from previous waves of technological change, in which labor shed from sectors replaced by automation was absorbed into new economic activities. For instance, the rise of the automobile industry destroyed industries dedicated to horse-based transportation but created vast new industrial and managerial employment in the auto industry, and earlier computerization created an abundance of high-skilled knowledge jobs, but, now, as human knowledge is transferred to machines through machine learning, machines become valuable substitutes for humans at multiple levels.[67] The "big data revolution" means that the data captured on knowledge-based occupations at the workplace and in the market may lead to direct automation of specific tasks and jobs. As algorithms generated by big data become predictable enough to make cognitive labor more and more redundant to a whole host of activities, from medical diagnosis to legal advice, it is clear that acquiring education and skills will no longer assure protection against job automation. Over time, we can expect a greater supply of knowledge workers simultaneous to a deskilling of their labor.

The end game in this process, although still far away, is *laborless production*. Writing in 1858 in the *Grundrisse*, the rough notes that he drafted for his magnus opus *Capital*, Marx anticipated this process. He speculated how machines and fixed capital would ultimately evolve into an automated system. "The means of labor passes through different metamorphoses, whose culmination is the *machine*, or rather, *an automatic system of machinery* . . . set in motion by an automaton, a moving power that moves itself. This automaton consists of numerous mechanical and intellectual organs, so that the workers themselves are cast merely as its conscious linkages." Automated machinery represents social knowledge transformed into assets controlled by capital. "The accumulation of knowledge and of skill, *of the general productive forces of the social brain*, is thus absorbed into capital, as opposed to labor. . . . In so far as machinery develops with the accumulation of society's capital, of productive forces generally, general social labor presents itself not in labor but in capital."[68]

The processes that push capitalism toward laborless production also *push marginal cost toward zero*, that is, zero cost for each incremental unit of output. As costs move toward zero, we step into the unknown. It is most unlikely that we will ever reach laborless production or zero marginal cost, much less in the near future (in any event, either situation would present capital with new contradictions, although here is not the place to elaborate). Nonetheless, these tendencies are underway, driven forward now by advanced digitalization, and are at least theoretically in the realm of the possible. Even if marginal cost never actually reaches nil, it is inexorably pushed down toward zero by the processes now underway. Digital capital in particular can become extremely cheap, e.g., software can be duplicated and distributed at almost zero incremental cost—and let us recall that practically anything can be digitalized, that is, codified, and once codified, then digitalized. Short of full automation, the ever-rising organic composition of capital (that is, the increase in fixed capital as machinery and technology relative to living labor) leads to more and more being produced with fewer and fewer precarious workers.

A 2017 United Nations report estimated that tens, if not hundreds, of millions of jobs would disappear in the coming years as a result of digitalization. The report also said that the spread of online labor platforms would accelerate a "race to the bottom of working conditions with an increasing precarity."[69] A 1998 study found that already in the late twentieth century some one-third of the global labor forces was under- or unemployed. Then in 2011, the ILO reported that 1.53 billion workers around the world, representing more than 50 percent of the global workforce, were in "vulnerable" employment arrangements. Eight years later, in 2019, it concluded that a majority of the 3.5 billion workers in the world either eked out a living (or attempted to) in the informal economy or worked in precarious arrangements, experiencing "a lack of material well-being, economic security, equality opportunities or scope for human development."[70]

Even before the pandemic hit, automation was spreading from industry and finance to all branches of services. Global sales of industrial robots were forecast to increase from 381,000 units in 2017 to 630,000 by the end of 2021.[71] We typically associate automation with factory work, but the latest wave has involved branches of the economy that were previously believed to be insulated from automation, such as fast food, agriculture, mining, and warehousing. One 2016 report from researchers at Oxford University concluded that up to 86 percent of jobs in restaurants, 75 percent of jobs in retail, and 59 percent of jobs in entertainment could be automated by 2035.[72] Artificial intelligence, robotics, and big data now underpin processes of mineral extraction, allowing for "digital mining" in which completely robotized trucks, shovels, and drills work around the clock. The fast-food industry is following the same path of automation. One startup, Miso Robotics, has been introducing "flippy," a robot cook that prepares and packages hamburgers, into quick-service restaurants in California, such as White Castle. Agriculture was already becoming automated before the pandemic, alongside a rapid concentration of corporate power in global agribusiness.[73] The agricultural robotics market expected to grow from $4.6 billion in 2020 to over $20 billion by 2025. "Overall, agricultural employment in California fell by about 11 percent in the first decade of the twenty-first century, even as the total production of crops like almonds, which are compatible with automated farming techniques, has exploded."[74] Driscoll's now employs Agrobot, a robotic strawberry picker in its California fields, and the California wine industry has reengineered the bulk of its vineyards to allow machines to span vines like a monorail and strip them of grape clusters or leaves. The pandemic hastened the turn toward agricultural automation and "digital farming" as the recruitment of seasonal agricultural workers became more difficult due to restricted movement.[75]

Beyond manual and low-skills service labor, automation and algorithms are expected to eventually replace much professional work, such as lawyers, financial analysts, doctors, journalists, accountants, insurance underwriters, and librarians. One robotics company, iRobot, has been working on creating robots that won't need to be programmed by high-skilled and high-paid engineers. The robots are to be taught and retaught to perform a task by shop floor workers who would need barely an hour of training to learn how to instruct the robots.[76] It may be that high-skilled professional jobs will be digitalized, while low-skilled and low-paid jobs requiring a low level of sensory motor skills, along with basic literacy and numeracy, will not be. Specifically, digital technologies are acquiring abilities previously exclusive to humans, such as pattern recognition and complex communication.

As mass industrial production took off in the late nineteenth century, capitalists introduced new forms of harsh discipline on shop floors, routinizing and deskilling work, as Harry Braverman, following Marx, discussed in his modern classic *Labor and Monopoly Capital*.[77] Bosses set out to separate thinking and conception from execution in the labor process. Workers were to provide their raw, degraded labor power, while conception would be concentrated in management, which would exercise total control over how tasks were carried out. "If the workers' exertion is guided by their own conception it is not possible," noted Frederick Taylor, the architect of "scientific management," "to enforce upon them the methodological efficiency of the working pace desired by capital."[78] However, management and supervisory work is not immune from digitally driven restructuring and is likely to be hit as hard as manual and professional occupations. Now in the wake of the pandemic accelerated digitalization may involve a gradual shift—or perhaps not so gradual—from management to computer algorithms.

As we have seen, technologies driven by artificial intelligence are becoming more widely adopted worldwide as a result of the conditions brought about by the contagion. The pandemic allowed the TCC to massively push forward capitalist restructuring that it could not previously accomplish because of resistance to the digital takeover. Those economic sectors bolstered by accelerated restructuring during the pandemic are where precarious forms of employment prevail, that is, the self-employed, contract, temporary, platform, and other such workers.[79] A growing portion of this proletariat labors by supplying "on-demand" digital services online, what is sometimes dubbed the "human cloud." The ranks of this digital proletariat will swell rapidly given the accelerated shift to online and home work. There appears to be a new bifurcation of work spurred on by the pandemic. There are, on the one hand, those who will shift to remote work. More than half of all employees in the United States were working at home in May 2020, whereas worldwide, according to the ILO, some 20 percent of employment may become permanently remote.[80] From their homes, these workers face new forms of control and surveillance. On the other hand, there are those locked into high-risk "essential" in-person work, such as health care providers, agricultural and industrial day laborers, cleaners, transport and delivery workers.

Capitalists will use mass unemployment along with more widespread remote and precarious work arrangements as a lever to intensify exploitation of those with a job, to heighten discipline over the global working class, and to push surplus labor into greater marginality. Tech work in China provides a glimpse into the Taylorist discipline and exploitation to which knowledge workers in the post-pandemic global economy will be increasingly subjected as they become precarious digital proletarians. Tech giants such as Huawei, Tencent, Alibaba, Baidu, and Xiaomi, among others, employ millions of college-educated workers, who are thrown into intense competition for a shrinking number of positions. Known simply as the "996 work regime," workers in China's expanding high-tech sector are forced to work from 9:00 a.m. to 9:00 p.m., six days a week. The strategy of Chinese and foreign-based transnational capital here seems to be one of combining an increase in absolute surplus value with that of relative surplus value. "The stereotypical image of privileged white-collar workers persists despite the changing employment reality and the decline and stagnation of white collar salaries," notes one labor activist in China.[81] As the number of skilled tech jobs contracts and unemployment expands around the world, the Chinese model is likely to be adopted elsewhere.

As the pandemic and its aftermath accelerates the process whereby labor is replaced by technology and algorithms, it is also bringing about significant change in the nature of the labor process itself. Lockdowns around the world forced nearly every industry and service at least partially online, giving the emerging tech-led bloc of capital newfound powers to mediate the gamut of human interaction in the economy and society. The pandemic lockdowns served as dry runs for how digitalization may allow the dominant groups to restructure space and exercise greater control over the movement of labor. Governments around the world, from India through South Africa to El Salvador, decreed states of emergency and violently repressed those who violated stay-at-home orders.[82] The lockdowns may have been necessary from the perspective of the health emergency, yet they showcased how the TCC and capitalist states may more tightly control the distribution of labor power, especially surplus labor, by controlling movement and by locking labor into cyberspace and, therefore, making it disaggregated and isolated. As new digital technologies expand the cognitive proletariat and the ranks of workers in the gig economy, they also allow for a stringent surveillance and control of this proletariat through cyberspace. This enhanced surveillance is, of course, matched by the heightened direct control over labor made possible by digital technologies. In 2018, for instance, Amazon secured patents for wristbands for use on warehouse workers to track their every move. The wristbands include tracking devices that monitor exactly where one's hands are in relation to inventory bins. They can track everything from how long a worker takes for a bathroom break to how much work is lost when one scratches her nose and can emit vibrations for infractions such as nose scratching and misplacing items.[83]

Well before the pandemic, digital restructuring had been making work more "modular." This refers to breaking work into smaller packets that are farmed out to workers by companies through platforms and online work. Such modulation takes to a new level industrial outsourcing associated with globalization in recent decades. "Work will increasingly get disconnected from companies, and jobs and work will increasingly get disconnected from each other," explained Ravi Kumar, the president of the India-based tech services conglomerate Infosys, which got its start in outsourced digital services. Some work will be done by machines, some will require physical proximity in an office or a factory, some will be done remotely, and some will be just a piece of a task that can be farmed out to anyone anywhere, he said. As more work becomes modular, digitized, and disconnected from an office or factory, noted Thomas Friedman, who interviewed Kumar on the future of modulation, "many more diverse groups of people—those living in rural areas, minorities, stay-at-home moms and dads and those with disabilities—will be able to compete for it from their homes." In Friedman's view, traditional education, such as universities, will disappear as workers acquire just enough skill to perform modulated tasks and no more. More than just privatized, education will more fully become the domain of the corporation itself, which will provide "in-house" and "just-in-time" learning suitable for modular tasks and nothing beyond that.[84]

Let us analyze what such digitally driven modulation means. The fragmentation of the labor process reaches new heights in post-pandemic global capitalism, insofar as the separation of conception from execution that Taylor called for deepens through digital restructuring and modulation. At this same time, the fragmentation of the work itself combines with the actual physical fragmentation of the members of the working class, that is, their physical isolation from one another. Workers experience further alienation from their own labor and its products, but also their alienation from one another is intensified as never before, both in the abstract and literally, in daily life. Collective labor is our very species being and the basis of our sociability. The switch to remote and online work breaks up awareness of our collective labor, as it becomes mediated through cyberspace and is spatially dispersed into individual isolated cubbyholes. The social, cultural, and psychological implications of this qualitatively new fragmentation of collective labor are vast.[85] Previously, work tasks may have been fragmented and deskilled, as physical and mental labor became separated, but workers still gathered together. Marx referred to cooperation in industrial capitalism as "the collective labor of many workers." He specifically described this collective labor as "agglomeration, heaping up of many workers in the same area" (in one place).[86] Such proximity allowed for awareness of common experience and, therefore, for the possibility of class consciousness, solidarity, and collective labor struggles. The physical isolation of more and more workers made possible by digitalization and brought on more extensively by the pandemic throws up great challenges for the struggle against capitalist exploitation and for class-based protagonism of the working class.

There is a generational dimension to these new conditions. Young workers born into the new capital-labor relations of fragmentation and precarity may have no consciousness of—or at least no direct experience of—earlier moments in these relations as a reference point. In the new capital-labor relation, gig workers are outsourced "independent contractors" deprived of labor rights and benefits embedded in the capital-labor relation forged in the earlier moments of redistributive capitalism and the "class compromise" of social democracy. Many gig workers have never even spoken to a person associated with the corporations for whom they work, as their labor is organized through automated platforms. Millions of such "freelancers" and "independent contractors" around the world found themselves suddenly without work as economies collapsed in 2020 and were not eligible for unemployment and other benefits accorded to workers internal to the corporate employment structure. Well before the pandemic, the leading corporations that exploit the labor of this outsourced precariat—especially the leading tech and platform firms, such Amazon, Uber, and Instacart—had little incentive to respond to the labor demands of their precarious workforce. This model is becoming more and more entrenched in the capitalist economy in the wake of the pandemic, with millions of newly unemployed people thrust into competition with one another and with those who managed to retain employment. This competition will increasingly play out remotely. Such isolation is not normal to our species. The danger is that it will become internalized as normal—that is, normalized. It is no wonder that the viral pandemic was associated with a worldwide spike in mental health problems and suicidal thoughts.[87]

The twentieth-century social contract that regulated work is a thing of the past for many, perhaps most of the millennial generation born between 1980 and the turn of century, and even more so the next generation that some have referred to as Generation Z. "Gen Z is uniquely prepared for the new era of social distancing, the online world, and sustainability," claimed the Bank of America report on the post-Covid economy cited in the previous chapter. "Other generations will be slow to adapt. Millennials, the 'double downgrade' generation, is most exposed to earning cuts as more US jobs have been wiped out this past month [April 2020] than have been created since the great financial crisis" of 2008.[88] New waves of labor are either forced into under- and unemployment or pushed into gig work in ever greater numbers. Online labor, especially its extreme expression in remote work, results in the further isolation and atomization of individuals who *objectively* remain involved in a collective labor process yet do not *subjectively* experience that process. The anti-collective and individualist tendencies inherent in social relations mediated by cyberspace are aggravated through such isolation.[89]

In conclusion, the new wave of worldwide digital restructuring that began in the aftermath of the 2008 financial collapse and is now turbocharged by the pandemic is resulting in a further fragmentation of the global working class. Fragmentation and isolation work against the development of class consciousness and collective political action as processes that require intersubjective formation. These processes force more and more proletarians to compete with one another. They expand the ranks of surplus labor and the downward pressure on wages and working conditions exerted by this reserve army of the un- and underemployed, but, more than that, they open up to exploitation by the TCC vast new reserves of labor that can be tapped into, tightly controlled, and disciplined in new ways. This is, of course, an entirely incomplete picture, one side only in a dialectical relationship. The other is the resistance of workers and the oppressed.

The global police state was on full display throughout the pandemic against restive populations thrown into chaotic situations as a result of the contagion and also against those who, notwithstanding the virus, took to the streets in countries around the world, from India to Chile, Thailand, and France, to protest the ongoing deprivations of global capitalism. The sustained uprising in the United States (and worldwide) sparked by the May 25, 2020, police murder in the US state of Minnesota of an unarmed black man, George Floyd, shined a spotlight on police state technologies deployed against millions of anti-racist protesters. In the repression unleashed against protests across the continents, the boundaries became blurred between active war zones and militarized cities experiencing civic strife. Digitally driven modalities of social control and repression have combined with a restructuring of space, allowing for new forms of spatial containment and control of the marginalized and the rebellious. Now, the boundaries that distinguish the domains of work and those of global police state are also becoming ever more blurred, as the pandemic and its aftermath expands the ranks of surplus labor, propels a general shift to home and remote work, and brings about the new digitally driven mechanisms of control over labor discussed above. In the next chapter I will explore how the global working and popular classes have attempted to revitalize their political action capacity under these new conditions and the challenges that they face in forging an emancipatory project.

CHAPTER THREE

WHITHER THE GLOBAL REVOLT?

"We are now in the phase of the 'autumn of capitalism' without this being strengthened by the emergence of 'the people's spring' and a socialist perspective."

—Samir Amin[1]

"There are decades when nothing happens; and there are weeks when decades happen."

—Bolshevik leader Vladimir Lenin

Times of crisis are times of rapid social change that open up the possibility of pushing society in many different directions, depending on the outcome of battles among contending social and class forces. In these times, prevailing ideologies break down, established ways of thinking lose their grip, new visions of what is possible come into view, and prospects for discontinuity and rupture capture the imagination. Instability generates insecurity and social anxiety, as fear and hope spread. But it also inspires people to think in new ways about the possibilities of radical change that are hard to imagine in times of stability and continuity. As the crisis of capitalist hegemony has deepened, socialism and even communism are back in the public discourse, especially among those born after the Cold War anti-communism and the collapse of the Soviet system. Marxism, so maligned not only by the ruling class but by the postmodernists and identitarian worldviews and politics, has drawn renewed interest, especially among young people. Sales of Marx's masterpiece of political economy, *Capital*, soared in the wake of the 2008 global financial collapse, as did sales of *The Communist Manifesto*.[2] Even mainstream pundits turned to Marx to help understand the Great Recession. In 2013, *Time* magazine ranked Karl Marx the fourteenth most influential figure in all of human history. That same year the prestigious science journal *Nature* reported that Marx is, by far, the world's most influential scholar of all time.[3]

The Pew Research Center has been conducting ongoing polls in the United States on views toward capitalism and socialism (of course, what people understand to be capitalism and socialism is not clear). According to its 2019 poll, a full 42 percent of US respondents had a favorable view of socialism, although the Pew poll did not break down responses by age groups. But a 2018 Gallup poll found that 51 percent of those aged eighteen to twenty-nine had a favorable view of socialism. Seen in historical context, another Gallup poll found that support for socialism stood at 25 percent in 1942 among the US population overall, and this increased to 43 percent in 2019. Revealingly, another poll found that support for socialism in the United States jumped by nearly 10 percent among young people during the 2020 pandemic.[4] This poll found that a full 60 percent of millennials and 57 percent of Generation Z supported a "complete change of our economic system away from capitalism." Worldwide, a 2020 poll found that a majority of people around the world (56 percent) believe capitalism is doing more harm than good. On a national level, according to the poll, lack of trust in capitalism was highest in Thailand and India (75 percent and 74 percent, respectively), with France close behind (69 percent). Majorities rejected capitalism in many Asian, European, Gulf, African, and Latin American countries. In fact, only in Australia, Canada, the United States, South Korea, Hong Kong, and Japan did majorities disagree with the assertion that capitalism currently did more harm than good.

The pandemic roused popular struggles from below as workers and the poor, after a brief pause in the global revolt as the world went into lockdown, engaged in new waves of strikes and protests as the contagion progressed. Prior to the outbreak, in fall 2019, the global revolt that broke out in the wake of the 2008 crisis reached a crescendo. From Chile to Lebanon, Iraq to India, France to the United States, Haiti to Nigeria, and South Africa to Colombia, mass struggles appeared in many instances to be acquiring a radical anti-capitalist character before the lockdown pushed protesters off the streets. But the lull was momentary. Within weeks of the lockdown protesters were out in force again despite the lockdown and the dangers of public congregation. There was a palpable radicalization taking place among workers and the poor, a heightened sense of solidarity within and across borders. In the United States, for instance, no fewer than one thousand strikes ripped across the country in the first six months of the pandemic. Workers mounted protests to demand their safety as the virus spread, while tenants called for rent strikes, immigrant justice activists surrounded detention centers and demanded the release of prisoners, auto, fast-food, and meat processing workers went out on wildcat stoppages to force factories to shut down, homeless people took over empty houses, and health care workers on the front lines demanded the personal protective equipment they needed to do their jobs and stay safe. For the most part, wildcat strikes were organized not by union leadership but from the grassroots.[5]

The ruling groups cannot but be frightened by the rumbling from below. Whether mass mobilization from below effects a fundamental change in the system of global capitalism, runs out of steam, is co-opted from above enough for the system to restabilize, or results, in the words of *The Communist Manifesto*, in "the common ruin of the contending classes" depends on a host of political and subjective factors than cannot be predicted beforehand. What *is* clear is that mass

popular struggles against the depredations of global capitalism are now conjoined with those around the fallout from the
pandemic. We have entered into a period of mounting chaos in
the world capitalist system. Capitalist crises are times of rapid
social change *precisely because* they generate intense social and
class conflict from below and from above.

Nonetheless, it is difficult to imagine that neoliberalism
as the predominant variant of world capitalism in the wake of
late twentieth-century capitalist globalization can be resus-
citated for long enough to allow for restabilization under the
pre-pandemic status quo. Neoliberalism simply does not have
any more reserves with which to contain financial chaos and
economic implosion.[6] The implacable drive to accumulation
will impede solutions to the crisis. Any economic recovery
will require more active state intervention in the economy and
regulation of the market. Renewed capitalist stability, if it can
even be achieved, would require a more profound restructuring—including the rebuilding of public sectors devastated by
forty years of neoliberalism—than the agents of financial and
corporate interests, along with the liberal and social democratic elite around the world, could possibly accomplish or
would even want to. Short of overthrowing the system, the
only way out of the crisis is a reversal of escalating inequalities
through a redistribution of wealth and power downward. That
will not come without a fight. The challenge for emancipatory
struggles is how to translate mass revolt into a project that can
challenge the power of global capital.

In chapter one, I analyzed how prior to the health emergency the global system was already headed toward a general
crisis of capitalist rule. Is it possible that we are entering a
prerevolutionary situation? The Bolshevik leader Vladimir
Lenin, whom I cited previously, described the *symptoms* of
what he called a revolutionary situation: 1) when there is a
crisis in the prevailing system, and it is impossible for the
ruling classes to rule in the old way; 2) when the want and

suffering of the oppressed classes have grown more acute than usual; 3) when, as a consequence, the masses increase their historical action. These symptoms are clearly upon us. Will their revolt develop into a struggle to overthrow the system once and for all? Masses of people engaged in now open, now veiled revolt are for the most part struggling not in pursuit of a larger political agenda of transformation, much less one that is guided by a theoretical understanding of capitalism and its crisis, but to resolve their most pressing problems of survival. The jump from a "revolutionary situation" to a revolutionary process requires other conditions not yet present, including a widespread belief that system change is attainable and worth fighting for, a revolutionary ideology and program, and organizations capable of leading the struggle for such change.

THE GLOBAL REVOLT I: SPRING AND BEYOND

In the months prior to the pandemic (and subsequent to Samir Amin's lamentation over the absence of a "people's spring"), a "global spring" broke out all around the world.[7] However, the 2019 spring was but a peak moment in popular insurgencies that spread in the wake of the 2008 Great Recession; a veritable tsunami of mass rebellion not seen since at least 1968. Social movements mounted sustained fightbacks against austerity, endemic corruption, authoritarianism and dictatorship, police violence, inequality, unemployment, corporate abuse, environmental degradation, and so on. The uprising had a truly global character. In Bangkok, a million people from the Red Shirts movement—so-named because the participants in the movement wear red shirts—took to the streets on March 14, 2010, against a state controlled by the military, the monarchy, and the moneyed elite. The Arab spring of 2011 set the Middle East and North Africa afire, resulting, among other things, in the overthrow of Egyptian dictator Hosni Mubarak in early 2011, in the face of an unremitting national insurrection. The Occupy Wall Street (OWS) movement that rallied under the now famous banner "We Are the 99 Percent!" started with the occupation of Zuccotti Park across the street from the New York Stock Exchange in September 2011 and spread to most major cities across the United States, before being violently suppressed in 2012. In Spain, in 2011, the *Indignado* (the indignant or the enraged) movement carried out similar occupations of public spaces and held no less than twenty-one thousand protests around the country against austerity and corruption, culminating in a march through Madrid on October 15 by half a million indignados.[8] The mass movements in Spain and Greece led to the creation of new left parties, Podemos and SYRIZA, respectively, which burst onto the political scene and contested power.

The *Financial Times* captured the mood in 2011 in a widely cited article penned by its lead commentator calling it "the year of global indignation":

> Is there such a thing as a global mood? It certainly feels like it. I cannot remember a time when so many different countries, all over the world, were gripped by some form of street protest or popular revolt. 2011 is turning into the year of global indignation.... popular revolt [is] breaking out across the globe. Europe has experienced political riots in Athens, sit-ins in Madrid and looting in London. In India, thousands of demonstrators turned out across the country to support Anna Hazare, a social activist and hunger striker, who has panicked the Indian government into agreeing to new anti-corruption measures. China has seen public demonstrations and online protests sparked by a factory accident and a high-speed train crash. In Chile, the past two months have seen huge marches by students and trade unions demanding higher social spending. In Israel, the main boulevards of Tel Aviv have been occupied by ordinary people protesting against the cost of living.[9]

In all of their diversity, these fights had—and have—a common underlying denominator: an aggressive global capitalism in crisis that is pushing to expand on the backs of masses who can tolerate no more hardship and deprivation. They also had demonstration effects on each other in this age of the internet and social media. The movements faced sustained state repression and a number of tragic reversals, epitomized by the seizure of power by a new dictatorship in Egypt that is perhaps even more repressive and totalitarian than its predecessor. After the initial worldwide wave, the protests ebbed and flowed but did not die out, with a fresh wave breaking out in 2017. In the two years leading up to the pandemic more than a hundred major anti-government protests swept the world, in rich and poor countries alike, toppling some thirty governments or leaders and sparking an escalation of state violence against protesters.[10] These protests involved students, prisoners and activists against mass incarceration, workers, often migrant workers, farmers, indigenous communities, democracy and anti-corruption activists, anti-racists, those struggling for autonomy or independence, anti-austerity campaigners, environmental advocates, and so on. What follows is an overview of some of the most notable protest movements that took place around the world in these two years.

Among the popular upheavals that garnered worldwide attention, the Sudanese revolution stands out. Protests began in December 2018 against the entrenched dictatorship of President Omar al-Bashir, who had been in power for thirty years, and continued with sustained civil disobedience for eight months. The protests started in response to the government's decision to end subsidies on essential food items but quickly evolved into a full-scale civil assault on the regime involving millions throughout the country. Fearful that the ruling groups would lose control, the military overthrew al-Bashir in a coup d'état in April 2019 and at the same time stepped up repression of the mass movement. On June 3, the military unleashed heavy gunfire and tear gas on peaceful protesters staging a sit-in in the nation's capital city, Khartoum, killing more than one hundred people, injuring hundreds more, and carrying out mass rape. In the aftermath of the massacre hundreds, perhaps thousands, were arrested. Yet the civil insurrection continued undeterred, with women playing a remarkable leadership role, giving the revolution an explicit feminist character. Crowds as large as half a million flooded the streets of the capital, with many camping outside of military headquarters. In poor neighborhoods, popular committees organized feverishly as dual power developed. By the end of the year, the military regime was forced to hand power over to a mixed military-civilian authority and promised elections within three years. It is far from clear if some form of democracy will actually be achieved—and how popular its content will be—or if the country will go the way of Egypt, but whatever the outcome the Sudanese people are unlikely to be pacified.[11]

In Latin America, Chile led the way in waves of popular mobilizations that reached a crescendo throughout the region in fall 2019. Known in Chile as the *estallido social* (social uprising), massive demonstrations, some of them a million strong, rocked the country that year and into 2020—right up until the outbreak of Covid-19. The triggering event for the civic uprising was the government's decision to increase subway fares in the capital city of Santiago. It came in the wake of nationwide student strikes from 2011 to 2013 demanding an end to privatized education and unequal access. The student movement quickly developed into a larger assault on the entire edifice of neoliberal capitalism, as workers and the popular classes engaged in the following years in ongoing strikes and protests. Chile has a vibrant and militant feminist movement, and, as in the Sudan, women were at the forefront of these struggles. The protests against the subway fare hike quickly snowballed into a sustained nationwide insurrection in the face of fierce police, army, and paramilitary repression that left several dozen dead, thousands injured, and thousands more arrested. The mass mobilization shifted the correlation of social and political forces against the neoliberal regime and forced the government to reverse the fare hike and promise reforms. It was forced to hold a referendum in the midst of the pandemic in October 2020 to convene a constitutional assembly to draft a new constitution—approved by an overwhelming majority. The historical and symbolic significance of the Chilean uprising did not go unnoticed by activists and protesters around the world. The 1973 coup d'état that overthrew the democratically elected socialist president Salvador Allende and brought to power the fascist dictatorship of General Augusto Pinochet ushered in the world's first experiment in neoliberalism and turned the country into perhaps the most "neoliberalized" in the world.

In France, what became known as the *mouvement des gilets jaunes* (yellow vest movement) for social and economic justice stormed the country starting in October 2018, coming as it did on the heels of years of mass mobilization against escalating inequality and austerity, and continued until the Covid-19 outbreak forced people off the streets. The most massive popular mobilization since 1968, already by the end of 2018 over 1,800 protesters and 1,000 police had been injured and the political climate irreversibly altered.[12] As elsewhere, where triggering events were often a government decision to raise the price of some essential item for populations already reeling from austerity and hardship, in France, the movement took off after the government decreed a rise in fuel prices. The yellow vest protesters—so named because the protesters wear the yellow vests that according to French law all motorists are required to keep in their vehicles in case of emergencies—moved beyond the immediate call for a rescinding of the fuel tax as the protests continued throughout 2019. They put forth a wide-ranging list of forty-two demands, among them a minimum wage increase, lower taxes on workers and pensioners, higher pensions, higher taxes on the rich, more social spending, cuts in politicians' salaries, environmental action, a plan for ordinary citizens to introduce referendums, and the nationalization of French corporations. On numerous occasions, strikes, marches, and roadblocks paralyzed Paris and other urban, suburban, and rural areas (the mobilizations were more territorial than workplace-based). One poll found that 80 percent of French people supported the movement, although not everyone agreed on all the demands, and as the movement became more militant some participating organizations dropped out. Nonetheless, after a brief lull during the lockdown, protesters were back on the streets in fall 2020.[13]

In China, labor resistance grew explosively during and after the 2008–2009 economic crisis. Prior to 2008, workers had waged spontaneous resistance, including petitions, roadblocks, and wildcat walkouts. These actions, in the words of one local labor organizer, "impacted both 'production discipline' and 'social order,' and made it difficult for capitalists to maintain an environment conducive for exploiting workers," in the wake of which the government implemented a series of labor control laws.[14] By the second decade of the century, students, intellectuals, and other allies of the labor movement had become involved in workers struggles. As elsewhere around the world, 2017–2019 become the flash point, with a fresh wave of nationwide actions in factories, services, construction, utilities, mines, and quarries, as workers protested backbreaking schedules, low pay, unpaid wages, and poor working conditions. In 2018, there were at least 1,700 recorded labor disputes on the mainland, up from 1,200 the prior year.[15] In Hong Kong, mass student-led protests throughout 2019 against China's authoritarian control captured world attention, before they died down in the face of repression and a centrifugal splintering of the movement (there appeared to be a hodgepodge of political and ideological orientations as well, with the US government financing the "pro-democracy" organizations leading the protests). International news media lost interest and largely ignored a more significant development in 2020 and onward, the rise of a new grassroots union movement and the forging of a more explicit working-class identity, as the unions targeted the housing shortage, high rents, inequality, low pay, and workplace health and safety.[16]

Meanwhile, back on the Chinese mainland, tech workers are becoming the new frontier or labor organizing. "A campaign-style, decentralized tech worker organizing, coordinated by workers and regions, indicates the potential of a new type of labor organizing," wrote one labor activist. As China became the "workshop of the world" in the late twentieth and early twenty-first centuries, the workers movement became grounded in export-oriented industry, based on a model of workers centers, or labor non-governmental organizations, that provided political support and organizational assistance to industrial workers. Industrial strike activity escalated and so too did state repression of the burgeoning workers movement. "As the worker central organizing model, which is adapted to organizing industrial workers, becomes increasingly unsustainable due to state repression, the tech worker organizing provides clues to a new model for worker mobilization that may hold particular advantages under the current political environment," observed Kevin Lin, referencing a March 2019 "virtual uprising" of tech workers.[17] While Lin was referring to China, the lessons hold true for other countries as millions join the ranks of degraded tech work under the precarious work conditions discussed in the previous chapter.

In India, in 2019 and 2020, hundreds of millions of workers, peasant farmers, and poor people participated in the two largest strikes in the world to date (as of this writing in early 2021), coming as they did on the heels of rolling mass protests in the preceding years, and upping the ante in the global class war unleashed by the TCC. At least 150 million workers took part in a January 2019 strike, under the umbrella of a joint committee of ten different trade union federations, a number of them under left-wing leadership. Leading the way were workers from transport, banks, financial services, public enterprises, power, steel, auto, and other industries, who were joined by student and farmer organizations. The twelve-point charter of demands included a national minimum wage, abolition of the contract labor system, trade union rights, social security coverage for all workers, and a halt to privatizations and to the anti-labor codes introduced by the government. To put the 150 million figure in perspective, about one in every fifty people on the planet participated in the strike!

Then, just two years later, on November 26, 2020, an even larger general strike paralyzed the country. An estimated 250 million workers and farmers joined together in a in a united front of over 250 organizations. To again put the 250 million number in perspective, if those who struck formed a country, it would be the fifth largest in the world after China, India, the United States, and Indonesia. Industrial belts across India came to a halt, and workers in the country's principal ports stopped work, joined by those from health care, services, telecommunications, mining, and transportation. They reiterated the twelve-point charter put forth by the trade unions two years earlier, called for a withdrawal of labor laws that extend the working day to twelve hours and that eliminate labor protections for unorganized workers, immediate relief for those suffering hardships due to the pandemic, and a reversal of privatizations and neoliberal policies. They also demanded the withdrawal of an agricultural bill introduced by the government that would open the floodgates to transnational agribusiness and devastate millions of farmers.[18] All this in the midst of the pandemic and in the face of fierce state repression, including the deployment of water cannons, tear gas, police and army barricades, and even live gunfire.

In the United States, in addition to the OWS movement mentioned above, some of the largest popular mobilizations in US history took place between 2008 and 2019, including: the 2017 Women's March that involved anywhere from three to five million people in numerous cities; the high school student–led March for Our Lives in 2018, which drew upward to two million people into the streets calling for gun control; the People's Climate March in New York City in 2014 and other environmental actions that drew in millions of people. Strike activity surged in 2018 and 2019 despite massive deunionization in recent decades (in 2019, some 10 percent of the workforce was unionized, down from 27 percent at the start of the neoliberal era in 1979). In those two years some one million workers engaged in major work stoppages—a nearly twenty-fold increase from the years immediately prior. Public school teachers led the way in a series of widely publicized strikes, followed by workers in the health care and auto industries, fast-food workers, and grocery store cashiers. It must be stressed, however, that these US government Bureau of Labor Statistics data include only information on work stoppages involving one thousand or more workers and at least one full shift, whereas 59.4 percent of private sector workers are employed by firms with fewer than one thousand employees.[19] Unregistered in official data were labor actions like the 2018 Google walkouts in protest over the company's handling of sexual harassment, involving thousands of workers, which did not last for one full shift, pickets by fast-food workers lasting a few hours, or the 2019 work stoppage by Uber drivers (part of a global day of action by ride-hailing workers), who are considered "independent contractors."

The anti-racist uprising in the United States sparked by the May 25, 2020, police murder in the city of Minneapolis of an unarmed black man, George Floyd, was possibly the largest and broadest mass action in US history, indicative of both the promise and the challenges of the global revolt. Bystanders recorded on their cell phones the brutal and callous murder, in which a police officer who had already restrained Floyd, placed him in handcuffs and laid him face down on the concrete, then proceeded to place his knee on the man's neck until the life was choked out of him, even as he cried out that he could not breath. Over the next several months an estimated twenty-five to thirty million people acting loosely under the banner of the Black Lives Matter (BLM) civil rights movement joined nationwide streets protests in some two thousand cities, large and small, in all fifty states, even in the midst of the pandemic. The uprising brought out people from all ethnicities and walks of life, indeed, many, perhaps a majority, of them white. The murder became a lightning rod for pent-up rage and despair over the mounting social crisis. Fearful of losing control, the ruling groups left no holds barred in unleashing the state's repressive apparatus against the largely peaceful protesters.

I participated in some of the marches in my city of residence, Los Angeles, and witnessed the use by militarized police and national guard units of tear gas, stun grenades, taser guns, pepper spray, rubber bullets, and batons against protesters. Curfews were imposed in dozens of cities, armored vehicles patrolled streets, and in at least one city, Atlanta, the armed forces deployed a column of tanks. At least ten thousand protesters were arrested, many kept for prolonged periods in indefinite detention, with three hundred charged with federal crimes, and at least thousand complaints lodged against instances of police brutality, excessive use of force, and rioting.[20] The uprising elicited a shift in the attitude of white workers toward police repression and racism, the historic scourge of working-class unity in the United States, as the percentage of white voters opposed to police racism climbed from 40 to 70 percent.[21] Solidarity actions and parallel anti-racist protests spread to over sixty countries around the world, including Nigeria, where demonstrators expanded their

Significant New Anti-government Protests in 2019 and 2020

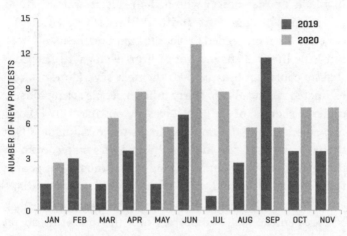

Source: *Global Protest Tracker, Carnegie Endowment for International Peace,* accessed December 11, 2020

protests into a larger movement targeting police and military repression, endemic corruption, and capitalist exploitation.

In all, it seemed like there were few countries not touched by the 2017–2019 tsunami, but evidence suggests that the rebellion escalated during the pandemic itself. The Carnegie Endowment for International Peace's "global protest tracker" recorded "significant antigovernment protests" in more than 110 countries from 2018 to 2020, involving over 230 major actions.[22] Given that the tracker recorded "over 100" such actions for the 2018–2019 two-year period, this would mean that 130 actions were recorded in 2020 alone (if, that is, the Endowment actually managed to accurately collect and record actions worldwide in the midst of the pandemic turmoil), or roughly a 160 percent increase during the first year of the pandemic over the average for the preceding two years. Covid-19 was, indeed, the lightning bolt before the thunder. "Just a few weeks after lockdowns were widely imposed, protests began to reemerge," noted the Endowment. "[A]lready in April [2020], the number of new protests rose to a high level;

approximately one new significant anti-government protest every four days."[23] It is crucial to recognize, however, that radicalization and mass mobilization have gone in both directions—left and right. The global backlash against capitalist globalization, as I will discuss below, has also fueled rising nationalism, much of it right-wing and regressive, including twenty-first-century fascist movements.

GLOBAL REVOLT II: QUANDARIES OF POPULAR STRUGGLES

"On July 24, 2020, Tesla's Elon Musk wrote on Twitter that a second US 'government stimulus package is not in the best interests of the people.' Someone responded to Musk soon after, 'You know what wasn't in the best interest of people? The U.S. government organizing a coup against Evo Morales in Bolivia so you could obtain the lithium there. Musk then wrote: We will coup whoever we want! Deal with it.'"

—Twitter exchange, as recounted by Vijay Prashad and Alejandro Bejarano[24]

The admonition issued by the US billionaire Elon Musk that "we" will overthrow any government that stands in the way of transnational corporate plunder brings home all of the sociopathy of a global capitalism in crisis that is pushing the world toward civil war. Musk was referring to an October 2019 coup d'état in Bolivia that overthrew the elected government of President Evo Morales. For five centuries the Andean nation has been a treasure trove for local and transnational elites, providing an endless stream of vital minerals for an expanding world capitalist system—first silver during the colonial era and in subsequent centuries tin, zinc, bismuth, antimony, tungsten, and petroleum gases, among others. The impoverished indigenous and mestizo masses waged decades-long—nay, centuries-long—struggles against the plunder and depredations of local and foreign capitalists and elites. These struggles came to a head in the so-called gas war early in the new century, sparked by the government's decision to privatize the national hydrocarbon company in a massive giveaway to transnational corporate investors. Strikes and blockades escalated in 2003, forcing the president to resign and flee the country. The victory only emboldened the mass movement, which three years later brought to power Evo Morales, the country's first indigenous president, and his Movimiento al Socialismo (Movement Toward Socialism: MAS) party. In response to the demands of the highly organized and mobilized population, the MAS nationalized hydrocarbon resources. It boosted public investment, redirected state revenues toward social programs, increased wages, and passed a new constitution that expanded autonomy and political participation for the country's indigenous majority.

The MAS came to power just as massive lithium reserves were discovered in the country. Until a few decades ago, lithium was a minor ingredient in lubricants and was also optionally alloyed with other minerals to make high performance alloys. With the digital revolution, however, lithium became a crucial resource for the global economy. Lithium is essential for electronic devices associated with computer and related technologies, such as smartphones, tablets, PCs, and laptops. As the key mineral used in electronic batteries it is at the very heart of the electronic-vehicle revolution and a critical resource for Musk's battery-driven Tesla car.[25] The demand for lithium was expected to double from 2020 to 2024, and Bolivia is estimated to have the world's largest known reserves.[26] As it set about to exploit the country's reserves, the Morales government welcomed transnational corporate investment in the industry but, nonetheless, set limits, all too unpleasing to the TCC, on foreign investment in the extraction and processing of the white metal. It was this concern over access to Bolivia's lithium that motivated Musk to embrace the US-backed coup d'état that ousted Morales.

To be sure, Morales's radical discourse disguised a more reformist program compatible with global capitalism. The MAS reached an accommodation with the country's landed elite and private sector in 2008—the same year as the Great Recession hit the global economy—in the face of a US-backed right-wing insurrection against its original radical impulse. As with other progressive governments that came to power in South America in the early twenty-first century, the MAS promoted a vast expansion of raw material production, agribusiness, and mega-infrastructure projects in partnership with foreign and local contingents of the TCC. It then taxed these operations to finance an expansion of social assistance programs, rather than pursuing a more fundamental transformation of property and class relations or a more direct challenge to the prerogatives of transnational capital. When commodities markets collapsed in the face of the global downturn, the contradictions of the model came home to roost, as progressive governments in the region lost power to a resurgent far right. In Bolivia, the MAS government faced mounting popular mobilization from below and from the left as discontent grew over the limits of its program and the giveaways to transnational capital, as well as over its clientelism and its moves to undercut popular control and autonomy at the grassroots level. In this context, local and transnational elites, backed by the United States, saw an opportunity to recover direct control of the state and unrestricted access to the country's labor and natural resources.

As the Bolivian case highlights, global capitalism is caught up in a new wave of predatory expansion. In particular, it underscores the predation of the new bloc of capital discussed in the previous chapter, as the TCC must seize resources to feed digitally driven expansion. On the one hand, transnational capital exercises enormous structural power over poor majorities. Even in instances such as South America, where the masses were politicized and well-organized, this structural power undercut efforts by states and social movements to undertake transformations that threatened the fundamental interests of the TCC. On the other hand, however, the Bolivian case highlights the difficulties that the ruling groups face in their effort to maintain control in the face of the global revolt that took off in the wake of the 2008 financial collapse. In fact, the far-right coup government was unable to hold on to power despite widespread repression and US support. It had to return governmental power to the MAS after mass protest forced it to hold elections in 2020.

Bolivia underscores the conundrum of the working and popular classes around the world as they struggle against the domination of the TCC and its political agents. How to translate mass revolt into a project that can challenge the power of global capital? Similar to the Latin American case, left-wing parties that contested state power on the heels of the Indignado movement in Spain and the anti-austerity uprising in Greece, where the SYRIZA party actually won government but found itself so constrained by the structural power of transnational capital and its local political agents that it was unable to make headway in its progressive agenda. In part, these reversals were (are) part of the dynamic of advances and reversals as struggles unfold between the masses from below and their rulers. But they also pointed to the quandaries of the left and the popular classes: underlying weaknesses and limitations that threaten to limit if not undermine the new round of mass rebellion unleashed in the wake of the pandemic.

In broad strokes, and with the usual precautions about generalizing (and as a further caveat, the following is but an overview of matters whose elaboration is best left for elsewhere), we can identify four quandaries that, far from mutually exclusive, are interwoven and synergistic. They must be seen as forming a larger unity in relation to global class struggle and civil war. *First*, there is an evident disjuncture between the proliferation of mass movements and popular uprisings around the world, on the one hand, and an organized and socialist-oriented left that could serve as a rudder to help steer these struggles into a larger transformative project, on the other hand. The institutional and party left has steadily lost power and influence in recent decades, as capitalist globalization and resistance to it has advanced, in part due to its own internal weaknesses and historic shortcomings and in part due to the centrifugal forces of capitalist globalization itself, insofar as it disaggregates and atomizes the exploited classes and their social and political spaces. The existing fragmentation and sectarianism that all too often pervades the left debilitates popular struggles at a time of planetary crisis. If the left is to be in a position to intervene effectively in the upheavals that are upon us, it must undertake the task of criticism and must urgently renovate a revolutionary project and a plan for refounding the state. At the same time as the socialist left is very weak, global union membership has steadily declined, so that even as working people everywhere rise up the majority of workers remain largely unorganized.

Everywhere, masses are feverishly challenging the powers that be in thousands of different social movements of every sort and under the most varied of circumstances. Any number of particular demands are put forward by these social movements and the popular sectors that become involved in them, but in order to fight back against global capitalism as the ultimate cause of the problems they seek to address, they must be aggregated into a larger emancipatory project, a program of action, and a strategy to push such a project forward. This requires political organizations that are able to articulate such a project in a double sense: articulate, as in link together and as in give voice to it. To take the case of the BLM-led civic uprising in the United States that took off in spring and summer 2020, millions of mostly young people yearning for radical change risked life and limb to participate, yet the protests showed a very low level of political development, with an organized left that could give it a more coherent anti-capitalist direction virtually nowhere to be seen and the politics of the youth lacking clarity, cohesion, and direction. There will be new mass uprising as surely as I write these lines in early 2021, yet the BLM movement became easy—and, for middle-class elements among it, willing—prey for co-optation by the powers that be, as I will discuss below. In the absence of a larger critique of the capitalist state, a left, and an alternative project, the movement died down as repression, co-optation, and fatigue took their toll.

As we saw, the crisis pushes the masses toward a radicalization, and many are coming to embrace the critique of capitalism and are open to the idea of socialism. At the same time, however, the stubborn identitarian paradigm that I discuss below has made many resistant to political organization and to identifying broader class interests beyond identity. We are missing what Gramsci referred to as a "Modern Prince"—a revolutionary political organization that can capture the imagination and build a counterhegemony to the capitalist state. Without political organizations and a program—without the unity of the spontaneous with organization—movements and mass actions over specific demands cannot be sustained and cannot mount a challenge to the system itself. In many places around the world the global spring and ongoing rebellions are semi-spontaneous outbursts that have found no left leadership that could guide them, no program that could sustain resistance and push it toward a more comprehensive project of change. "Neglecting, or worse still despising, so-called 'spontaneous' movements, i.e., failing to give them a conscious leadership or to raise them to a higher plane by inserting them into politics, may often have extremely serious consequences," warned Gramsci. "It is almost always the case that a spontaneous movement of the subaltern classes is accompanied by a reactionary movement of the right-wing of the dominant class, for concomitant reasons." Indeed, this is precisely what appears to be playing out, as we will discuss below; the far right is gaining ground rapidly.

Second, as I noted in chapter one, economic globalization takes place within a nation-state-based system of political authority. Capitalist state power is scattered into some two hundred nation-states, and transnational state apparatuses are unable to exercise any real political authority over the global system as a whole. This gives transnational capital enormous structural power over individual nation-states and over the global economy. Capitalism was from its inception a world system. If socialism in one country was impossible in the twentieth century, it is even more so impossible in this age of capitalist globalization. The space for alternative projects at the national level has dramatically constricted over the past half-century. Social democracy sought to regulate the capitalist economy in order to capture and redistribute some surplus into social programs and guide capital accumulation toward some broader social aim besides profit-making, but social democracy exists now little more than in name. François Mitterrand, a left-leaning social democrat, was elected to the French presidency in 1981 with a program to greatly expand the public sector, raise wages, extend social spending, raise taxes on capital, and nationalize the banks and several major industrial groups. But the corporate elite launched a capital strike and withdrew billions of dollars from the country, resulting in a rapid deterioration of the economic situation. Mitterrand was forced to do an about-turn and by 1983 had embraced monetarism, neoliberalism, and austerity.[27]

That the social democratic project in France, one of the most developed countries in the world, was brought down early on in the neoliberal era by the TCC brings home the point that projects of radical redistribution, not to speak of socialism, are increasingly impossible in a single country, much less in small, vulnerable countries like Bolivia or Greece. Struggles at the nation-state level are far from futile. Moreover, mass struggles unfold at the level of each nation-state; the only state power the masses *can* seize is that of the nation-state. As the Greek socialist theoretician Nicos Poulantzas noted, the state—in this case, *specifically* the national state—is the *point of condensation* for tensions in the social order and the political system (in Poulantzas's own words, the state "is the specific material condensation of a relationship of force among classes and class fractions").[28] Yet the national state is unable to meet both the demands of popular sectors from below and the imperative of assuring the accumulation of capital.

This contradiction, as I discussed earlier, throws national states into spiraling crises of legitimacy. As capitalist globalization deepens, the state cannot resolve this contradiction and must step up its repressive control over the working and popular classes, which includes efforts at co-optation and passive revolution (see below). For these classes, struggles at the level of the nation-state must be part of a more expansive transnational counterhegemonic project, including transnational trade unionism, transnational social movements, and transnational political organizations that put forth a *transnational* transformative project—a unified minimal program coordinated across borders and across regions. This holds true as much for a global Keynesianism, that is, a project of transnational redistribution and regulation of the global economy—or, if you will, a global social democracy—as it does for a global socialism. In sum, emancipatory struggles in the age of global capitalism *must* be *simultaneously national and transnational*—must identify and prioritize the class antagonisms within *and across* countries and regions

There have been important attempts in recent years to establish transnational forums of struggle beyond nineteenth- and twentieth-century internationals of left political parties. Delegates from some 150 countries representing several thousand social movements and radical organizations came together in early 2001 under the banner "another world is possible" to form the World Social Forum (WSF) as an umbrella "movement of movements," representing an important milestone in the construction of a global popular counterhegemony. But the WSF lacked a coherent strategy for challenging global capitalism. The multitude of forces that made up the forum were divided over numerous issues: between those calling for reform of the system and those searching for ways to replace it altogether; between those emphasizing negotiation with global elites and those seeking mass mobilization and confrontation. Moreover, the WSF explicitly rejected the idea of a united political program across borders to which all would commit—in fact, it rejected outright the idea of political programs—and also explicitly prohibited political parties from being a part of the Forum, thus contributing to the separation of left political parties from mass social movements. It also rejected "violence," so organizations like the Zapatistas in Mexico were excluded.

In early 2019, leftists and activists from around the world took an important step forward in the transnationalization of popular struggles, launching the Progressive International, in what could arguably be considered the successor to the WSF. The new organization set up a more formal structure for individuals and organizations—including political parties—to become members, set about drafting a blueprint for a common platform of struggle across borders, and committed to participating across borders in social justice campaigns around the world.[29] There are other signs of growing transnational coordination of popular and working-class struggles, including transnationally coordinated strikes by Uber drivers in 2019 and Amazon workers in 2020 that spanned dozens of countries.[30]

However, the national state as a point of condensation, or a lightning rod, for tensions and contradictions in the social order and the political economy presents the left and popular forces with other problematic implications for transformative and emancipatory projects. A brief theoretical excursion is useful. As I mentioned in chapter one, the problem of the relationship between capital and the state is rooted in a more expansive theoretical matter, that of the relationship of the political to the economic in the capitalist system. Unlike earlier class societies, the separation of the political from the economic under capitalism is *formal* insofar as capitalists, as the economically dominant class, are not necessarily in *direct* control of the state machinery, and we have numerous instances around the world in recent years of progressive and even anti-capitalist forces winning national state power, from Salvador Allende in Chile from 1970–1973 to the more recent cases of Bolivia and Greece. As I mentioned above, these forces come under pressure to conform to the interests of transnational capital. These pressures are applied especially through global financial markets, although we must also not forget direct coercive pressure applied by the political and state agents of global capitalism, such as with the 2019 coup d'état in Bolivia or campaigns of destabilization against Venezuela and Cuba. This separation is taken as natural or organic in liberal ideology and in Weberian sociology; political and economic structures are seen as separate spheres, each with its own innate laws and dynamics, the first pursuing power and the second wealth.

In historical materialist approaches, this *formal* or apparent separation of the political and the economic spheres of a larger social totality under capitalism is not real; it is illusory. Expanding our theoretical excursion, throughout the history of class societies going back some eight thousand years, the economically dominant classes exercised direct control of the state in pursuit of their class interests. Slave-owning and feudal aristocracies directly controlled the slave and feudal states. In capitalism, however, there is a formal separation of economic control from political power. The analytical distinction between political and economic structures or spheres corresponds to their institutional separation under capitalism. The economy becomes a "private" sphere in which the power to expropriate the social product, to extract surplus value, has been privatized, and people are decidedly unequal and subordinated to the market. This economic sphere is removed from the "public" or governmental sphere and appears to relate externally rather than internally to the "public" sphere of the state, in which people are equal juridical citizens, and in which leftists can run for and even win office. One does not vote under capitalism for who will own property or for how property is distributed; such material (economic) relations are removed from the public sphere. Moreover, this public sphere is not directly implicated in the private appropriation of the surplus product, that is, in capitalist profit-making. Yet the state is charged with organizing the general conditions of accumulation, for its existence and its legitimacy is dependent upon a vibrant economy, that is, upon the reproduction of capitalist production relations, or the capital-labor relation. The state exercises its autonomy from the directives of capitalists as individuals, as groups, or as fractions, but it is not autonomous from those relations. Herein lies the *underlying unity* of politics and economics, as well as the institutional separation of the political and the economic spheres—that separation being a very consequence of the establishment of capitalist production relations.[31]

This separation takes the expression of the separation of the "public" from the "private," the former seen as the state proper, or what Gramsci referred to as "political society," and the latter as what Gramsci referred to as "civil society." In his essay, "State and Civil Society," Gramsci critiques the conception of the state developed by ideologues of capitalist society as derived from the separation of politics and economics and "conceived as a thing in itself, as a rational absolute."[32] This results, in Gramsci's view, in a reified or fetishistic view, in which individuals "are led to think that in actual fact there exists above them a phantom entity, the abstraction of the collective organism, a species of autonomous divinity that thinks, not with the head of a specific being, yet nevertheless thinks, that moves, not with the real legs of a person, yet still moves." Gramsci criticized this view of the state as a "thing-in-itself," as an entity unto itself in political society and above the social and power relations in civil society and the economy, as "statolatry." Instead, the state is "the entire complex of practical and theoretical activities with which the ruling class not only justifies and maintains its dominance, but manages to win the active consent of those over whom it rules."[33] Here the state becomes the "integral" or "extended" state, in Gramsci's formula, encompassing political plus civil society, a conception aimed at overcoming the illusory dualism of the political and the economic.

Now, we can link this theoretical excursion to the problem at hand, the second of the four quandaries I am discussing here. Popular struggles that target the state as the point of condensation for tensions and contradictions that originate in the political economy of capitalism run the risk of dissolving class-based demands of the proletariat and other exploited classes into more abstract demands for democratization of the state, often merely representation in public institutions, along with an end to corruption.[34] Radical mobilization from below runs the risk of being channeled into the state's institutional processes, co-opted into an agenda of liberal reform that does little to challenge the social order. Indeed, they can strengthen the hegemony of dominant groups as these groups accommodate liberal demands for equality of representation and inclusion in the capitalist state and its institutions. In these circumstances the class identity of movements of the working and popular classes becomes an abstract designation as "people" or "citizens," as under capitalism citizens enjoy political equality even as they experience explicit inequality in the economy. The paradox of the capitalist system under formally democratic arrangements is just that: political equality before the state, on the one hand, and socioeconomic dictatorship in the economy, on the other. Yet masses of people are able to see the state more easily than they see capital, as the state becomes the point of condensation for social and economic grievances, at a time when the capitalist state has a radically diminished capacity to meet the demands from below in the face of the crisis.

The case of the 2020 anti-racist uprising in United States is illustrative of the dilemma. The movement targeted the police as the visible front line of the capitalist state. It is the police who carried out the extrajudicial execution of George Floyd. It is the police who come into direct contact with the dispossessed and the marginalized and are responsible for controlling them. Capitalists and elites whose wealth and power are protected by the police do not go into the streets to confront poor black people and workers; they command quietly from corporate boardrooms, banking and financial houses, foundations, and government offices. We cannot do away with police violence and mass incarceration in the United States without doing away with surplus labor, that is, doing away with the system that relegates tens of millions in the United States (and several billion worldwide) to the margins as surplus humanity. As we saw previously, the top 1 percent of humanity owns over half of the world's wealth, and the top 20 percent own 94.5 of that wealth, while the remaining 80 percent have to make do with just 5.5 percent. Such savage social inequalities are politically explosive, and to the extent that the system is unable to reverse them it turns to ever more violent forms of containment to manage immiserated populations. The police are a coercive instrument of the capitalist state to control surplus labor, the poor, and the working class. In the United States, workers from racially oppressed groups disproportionately swell the ranks of surplus labor and the immiserated population.

In the United States, workers and poor people escalated their struggles at the start of the Covid-19 pandemic. As I noted above, in Amazon warehouses, meatpacking and auto plants, supermarkets, hospitals and nursing homes, they undertook a wave of strikes and protests as the coronavirus spread to demand safe working conditions and hazard pay (note that these frontline and essential workers come disproportionally from racially oppressed communities), while tenants called for rent strikes, immigrant justice activists surrounded detention centers and demanded the release of prisoners, and homeless people took over homes. Yet there was a *debilitating disconnect* between these worker-led struggles in the capitalist economy and the black youth–led anti-racist uprising. The secret to moving forward the mass anti-racist struggle was to link it with the mass working-class struggles that were simultaneously breaking out in 2020, and in this way to have targeted the roots of racism in capitalist exploitation, or at least to link this anti-racist struggle with those worker struggles, but this did not happen, at least not in the 2020 conjuncture. The anti-racist uprising surged for several intense weeks as the major urban centers became battlegrounds between protesters and the police state, but the protests fizzled out as repression, co-optation, and fatigue took their toll, and as the dominant groups turned to incorporating the BLM movement into the hegemonic order.

The two quandaries we have discussed so far form a unity. Mass movements generated by the very contradictions and deprivations of the capitalist system target the state as the point of condensation. The absence of radical political organizations and a socialist left makes it difficult for these movements to move from a struggle for democratization (especially equality of representation and inclusion) and demands for redistribution to a larger attack on the economic system and capitalist relations of production. But there was more at work here. Why was (is) the language of class so

absent? The two quandaries in their unity cannot be separated from the *third*, the influence, even hegemony, over mass
struggles of identitarian paradigms that, rather than enhance,
have *eclipsed* the language of class and the critique of capital
and political economy.[35] These paradigms did not develop in
a vacuum. They emerged in the late twentieth century out of
the collapse of the old Soviet bloc, the defeat of the left, the
demise of Third World nationalist and revolutionary projects,
and the repression of radical working-class struggles. The
triumph of neoliberalism found its philosophical alter ego in
a postmodernism that undermined ideas of broad solidarity,
working-class struggle, and socialist projects.[36]

A key part of the story here, in my view, is the betrayal
of the intellectuals, for no struggle of the oppressed can be
without its organic intellectuals, and the battles to come are
as much theoretical and ideological as they are political. Many
intellectuals who previously identified with anti-capitalist
movements and emancipatory projects withdrew into an identitarian politics of reform and inclusion, a set of political and
cultural practices, radical only in language, that are at best
liberal and that end up shoring up the hegemony of capital. It
was the mass struggles of the 1960s and 1970s themselves that
helped representatives from the oppressed groups to join the
ranks of the professional strata and of the elite. In academia, it
opened up space for a new intellectual petty bourgeoisie whose
class aspirations became expressed in postmodern narratives
and identitarian politics, while in the larger society it found
resonance among aspiring middle-class and professional/
managerial elements that sprung from the mass movements.
If radical ideas only become a historical force when they are
channeled into political organization, into a vision of a new
world and a revolutionary project to bring it about, the same
is true for all ideas, revolutionary or otherwise; they become a
material forces when they influence mass consciousness and
action. To Marx's observation that "theory itself becomes a

material force when it has seized the masses," political scientist Adolph Reed has added: "Ideology is the mechanism that harmonizes the principles that you want to believe with what advances your material interests."[37]

As post-modern narratives became hegemonic in the academy and in the broader society they shaped the common sense understanding of racial, gender, and other forms of oppression. Identitarian politics should *not be confused* with struggles against particular forms of exploitation and oppression that different groups face. Ethnic, racial, gender, and sexual oppression are not tangential but constitutive of capitalism. There can be no general emancipation without liberation from these forms of oppression. But the inverse is just as critical: all the particular forms of oppression are grounded in the larger social order of global capitalism that perpetually regenerates these oppressions. The anti-Marxism of identitarianism is alienating a generation of young people from embracing a desperately needed Marxist critique of capitalism at the moment of its globalization. In these narratives, Marxism became a "Eurocentric/Western-centric ideology." The claim that the European origin of Marxism makes it "Eurocentric" and inherently limited involved a rejection of any universalism. In its place was a universe of particulars and the celebration of "differences" and fragmentation (into essentialized identities and single-issue social movements), so that there is no underlying principle of human social existence, no collective subject capable of social transformation, indeed no emancipatory project that could unite a majority of humanity. All forms of "resistance" to *oppression* were celebrated but *exploitation* was banished from the popular vocabulary. Any understanding of *exploitation* requires the tools of Marxist political economy, yet this was maligned a "class reductionism," a "metanarrative" of (white, male) Westerners, and "economism," such that any underlying structural causes of oppression could not be identified.

Notwithstanding its often radical-sounding language, as the identitarian approach eschews class and the critique of capitalism at the level of theory and analysis, it advances the class politics of the petty bourgeoisie. The most such a politics can aspire to is symbolic vindication, diversity (often meaning diversity in the ruling bloc), nondiscrimination in the dominant social institutions, and equitable inclusion and representation *within* global capitalism. It is no wonder that alongside the economic restructuring of capitalist globalization since the 1980s, the emerging TCC responded at the cultural level to the popular and revolutionary uprisings of the 1960s and the 1970s by embracing as its own "diversity" and "multiculturalism" as a strategy to channel the struggle for social justice and anti-capitalist transformation into nonthreatening demands for inclusion, if not outright co-optation, and in this way to reconstruct capitalist hegemony. The strategy served to derail ongoing revolts from below. The ruling classes managed to accommodate what contentious politics flowed from the identitarian paradigm. The strategy aimed to neuter through co-optation the demands for social justice and anti-capitalist transformation. Dominant groups would now welcome representation in the institutions of capital and power but would suppress, violently if necessary, struggles to overthrow capital or simply curb its prerogatives. Some among the historically oppressed groups gained representation in the institutions of power; others aspired to do so.

To return to the matter of anti-racism in the United States, there was a felicitous meeting of aspiring professional/managerial and middle-class elements from below with the ruling groups from above around the new "racial justice" agenda. The dominant groups now funded and championed the conception of racism put forth by a new "anti-racist" politics as bias, personal aggression, racial disproportionality in the distribution of rewards and penalties, and a lack of inclusion and representation.[38] Opposition to racism as personal injury and "micro-aggressions" eclipsed any critique of the macro-aggressions of capitalism and the link between class exploitation and racial, gender, and other forms of oppression. As one report put it:

> The contemporary period, marked by rising racism and widespread political disarray, has also seen the emergence of jargon and terms that place individual racism and antiracist strategies at the center, developed and promoted by a cottage industry of professional antiracist outfits, media platforms, and academics. Whether "racial awareness" or "unconscious bias," "white privilege," "white fragility" or "micro-aggressions," each concept is premised on an individualized form of racism that is cut off from any structure of power, framing it as a nebulous, free-floating form of oppression that can be diagnosed and treated by individualist interventions.[39]

The 2020 anti-racist uprising discussed above evidenced the result of such a politics and consciousness. Devoid of any critique of capitalist exploitation that linked race to class, it was swiftly co-opted from above and from within. The protesters focused on disproportionate police violence against racially oppressed communities and called for defunding police departments. Yet racist police are an extension of the capitalist state. They exist to defend property from the propertyless, to enforce the power of capital and the rich over the poor and dispossessed majority who, in the United States, come disproportionately from racially oppressed communities. In the big picture, the solution was (is) not to reform law enforcement, since law enforcement means enforcing a legal system that under capitalism is intended to protect the rich and the powerful from the poor and the dispossessed through criminalization of the latter or simply through enforcement of property rights. From 2015 to 2019, a total of 4,885 people in the United States were shot and killed by the police, 1,295 of those black, compared to 2,471 white.[40] The rate that blacks were killed by police is more than twice the rate for whites, since blacks constitute 13 percent of the US population but account for over 26 percent of those killed, and this disproportionality became the focus of the "racial justice" agenda with regard to police violence. Yet the greatest danger to black lives comes from the economic violence of capitalism, which takes hundreds of thousands of black (and other) victims of unemployment, occupational hazards, malnutrition, substandard housing, homelessness, lack of access to health care, exposure to toxic wastes, and so on. More than five thousand workers die on the job every year as a result of work injuries, the majority of them preventable, and another fifty to sixty thousand die each year due to occupational diseases (worldwide nearly three million workers die on the job every year).[41] Predictably, blacks are overrepresented in this group,[42] not because of racial discrimination per se, but because they are overrepresented in the most hazardous (and least remunerated) occupations.

Beyond the demand for police reform, young people in the streets came to center their protagonism on little else than eradicating the *symbols* of racism and oppression. They upturned statues and monuments of historical figures and cultural icons associated with the history of racism. Upturning monuments is an act of symbolic or discursive justice that by itself is not a fundamental threat to the system, so long as these acts can be isolated from demands for more fundamental social and economic transformation, which is why they were quickly embraced by many political and corporate elites. Changing the names of military bases that are often named after racist historical figures, as the protesters demanded, may have been satisfying in terms of symbolic justice, yet it did not change the fact that these bases housed military forces that exist to intervene around the world on behalf of capital and empire, and that blacks are overrepresented in the military, because they are overrepresented in the ranks of surplus labor and enjoy the least opportunity for satisfying employment in the civilian economy.

The powers that be embraced the language of struggle against "systemic racism" as the phrase became emptied of any real meaning. Political and economic elites touted their commitment to "racial justice." CEOs of major global banks and corporations whose policies perpetuate racial inequality "took the knee" and declared their "solidarity" with aggrieved communities, as did Democratic and Republican Party stalwarts, as they attempted to commodify and convert "black lives matter" into a corporate logo.[43] "Racial justice" became big business and a purse string for the aspiring black middle class and elite toward whom flowed millions of dollars from corporations and the foundations they fund. In the wake of the mass uprising state, corporate, and foundation donors and rich individuals committed a mind-boggling $10 billion to BLM-related causes, according to the *Economist*.[44] The campaign from above *and from within* aimed to marginalize the radical anti-capitalist impulse and to promote black capitalism and professional development, to channel the uprising away from working-class struggle and into lobbying, electoral demands, professional development, and inclusion.[45]

The theme of co-optation by capitalist philanthropy was first raised by Marx and Engels, who wrote in *The Communist Manifesto* that a sector of the capitalist class is "desirous of redressing social grievances in order to secure the continued existence" of its rule.[46] In his study *Under the Mask of Philanthropy*, Michael Barker shows how the politics of capitalist philanthropy is aimed at deflecting challenges to the system:

> Reform or revolution? This is a question that is central to effective progressive social change. From many people's point of view there is little doubt that capitalism must be eradicated, so the only question that

remains is "how might this revolutionary process proceed? Revolutionary action does not negate reform, as radical reforms are a critical part of any socialist praxis of change. On the other hand, liberal reforms without revolutionary direction are unlikely to build the momentum that will be necessary to oust capitalism. Thus understanding how leading activists and intellectuals who were formerly committed to revolutionary social change give up on such principles and dedicate their lives to moderating capitalist oppression is critical for social and political movements seeking to resist such challenges.[47]

In the larger analysis, the ruling groups attempt what the Italian communist Antonio Gramsci referred to as passive revolution: efforts by dominant groups to bring about mild change from above in order to defuse mobilization from below for more far-reaching transformation. Integral to passive revolution is the co-optation of leadership from below and the integration of that leadership into the dominant project. Gramsci also referred to this process as *transformismo*, in which rule by the dominant groups is dependent on the ongoing absorption of intellectual, political, and cultural leaders of the subordinate majority into the ruling bloc and the resulting decapitation and disorganization of resistance from below.[48] "The more a dominant class is able to absorb the best people from the dominated classes," Marx noted, "the more solid and dangerous is its rule." Passive revolution comes into play at times when the system faces an impending crisis of hegemony. Whenever the hegemony of the bourgeoisie begins to disintegrate and a period of organic crisis develops, the process of reform or reorganization that is needed to reestablish its hegemony will to some extent have these characteristics of passive revolution.

If identitarianism leads to a dead end, so too does its close cousin nationalism, which obliterates class by establishing a unified identity for citizens of a particular country. In the core countries of world capitalism there has been a resurgent nationalism that is often racist, chauvinistic, and xenophobic and ends up serving far-right agendas. Elsewhere around the world, a revolutionary nationalism that was a central part of anti-imperialist and anti-colonial struggles in the preceding two centuries has become a conservative force in the age of globalized capitalism. "There is no compelling evidence that nationalists are the natural allies of the working class, regardless of the objective class position of any nationalist," notes international relations scholar Hilbourne Watson. "Nationalists do not see a problem with local capitalists exploiting workers; however, they seldom recoil from decrying exploitation by foreign capitalists, in effect making the nationality of capital, rather than the exploitation of man by man, the real problem. The fact that capital accumulation is a global process makes the nationality of capital secondary."[49] Watson notes that liberation from the exclusionary loyalties of collective identities "is precisely what makes progress possible in history." What is possible is "an open-ended political project as part of a continuous process from which we are inclined to recoil because it beckons us to part with certain illusions that make us fearful of 'falling off the cultural edge of one's world and its self-understanding.'"[50]

THE THREAT OF FASCISM AND A GLOBAL POLICE STATE

The *fourth* quandary that mass struggles from below face is the threat presented by far-right strongmen and authoritarian and fascist projects that, animated by the ongoing crisis, compete for support among the popular and working classes. There has been a rapid political polarization in global society since 2008 between this insurgent far right and an insurgent left. Both far-right and left forces appeal to the same social base of those millions who have been devastated by neoliberal austerity, impoverishment, precarious employment, and relegation to the ranks of surplus labor, all greatly aggravated by the pandemic. Yet the far right has often been more effective in recent years than the left in mobilizing disaffected populations and has made significant political and institutional inroads. There is a paradox here in need of explanation. Many of the strongmen and fascist-leaning leaders, such as Philippine president Rodrigo Duterte or Indian prime minister Narendra Modi, enjoyed high approval ratings at the same time as they pushed forward policies that hurt workers and the poor and unleashed repression against opposition forces. Charismatic fascists such as former US president Donald Trump and Brazilian president Jair Bolsonaro garnered genuine mass support. Duterte's approval rating soared to some 90 percent in late 2020, even as the economy contracted sharply, while Modi enjoyed an overall 55 percent approval rating in the midst of national crisis and mass strikes involving hundreds of millions of people.[51] Trump's approval ratings never surpassed the 50 percent mark, and although he failed in his 2020 bid for reelection, he nonetheless won 74 million votes—this despite his government's all-out attack on workers and utter disregard for the poor.

This paradox reflects, in part, the polarization between left and right that I observed. But there is a larger story that requires, first, an excursion into the nature of this authoritarianism and fascism. Although we cannot collapse authoritarianism and fascism into one despite their affinity, both must be explained by the crisis of global capitalism. I have been writing about the rise of twenty-first-century fascist projects around the world since 2008.[52] In the broader picture, fascism is *a particular response to capitalist crisis*, such as that of the 1930s and the neofascist movements that took off in the aftermath of the 2008 financial meltdown. Trumpism in the United States, BREXIT in the United Kingdom, the increasing influence of neofascist and authoritarian parties and movements throughout Europe (including Poland, Germany, Hungary, Austria,

Italy, Holland, Spain, Great Britain, Denmark, France, Belgium, and Greece)[53] and around the world, such as in Israel, Turkey, Colombia, the Philippines, Brazil, and India, as distinct as they may be from one another, have in common that they represent far-right responses to the crisis of global capitalist hegemony. The social bases of fascism and strongman rule are made up of masses who face destabilization and insecurity in the face of capitalist globalization, and who have been mobilized from above by the manipulation of fear and the promise to alleviate rising social anxiety and restore stability. The key to the neofascist appeal is this promise to avert or reverse downward mobility and social decay and to restore some sense of stability and security. As popular discontent has spread, far-right and neofascist mobilizations have played a critical role in the effort by dominant groups to channel mass discontent away from a critique of global capitalism and toward support for the TCC agenda dressed in populist rhetoric.

Fascism seeks to rescue capitalism from its organic crisis, that is, to violently restore capital accumulation, establish new forms of state legitimacy, and suppress threats from below unencumbered by democratic constraints. As with its twentieth-century predecessor, the project hinges on the psychosocial mechanism of displacing mass fear and anxiety at a time of acute capitalist crisis toward scapegoated communities, whether Jews in Nazi Germany, immigrants in the United States, Muslims and lower castes in India, Palestinians in Palestine/Israel, Rohingya in Burma/Myanmar, or the darker-skinned and disproportionately impoverished population in Brazil, and also onto an external enemy, such as communism during the Cold War or China and Russia currently. The project involves a fusion of repressive and reactionary state power with a fascist mobilization in civil society. Twenty-first-century fascism, like its twentieth-century predecessor, is a violently toxic mix of reactionary nationalism and racism. Its discursive and ideological repertoire involves extreme nationalism and the promise of national regeneration, xenophobia, and doctrines of racial/cultural supremacy, alongside a violent racist or ethnic mobilization, martial masculinity, millennialism, militarization of civic and political life, and the normalization, even glorification, of war, social violence, and domination.

The appeal to fascism offers workers from the dominant racial, ethnic, or national group an imaginary solution to real contradictions: recognition of the existence of suffering and oppression, even though its solution is a false one. Yet in this age of globalized capitalism there is little possibility of providing such benefits, so that the "wages of fascism" appear to be entirely psychological. The ideology of twenty-first-century fascism rests on irrationality—a promise to deliver security and restore stability that is emotive, not rational. It is a project that does not and need not distinguish between the truth and the lie, which helps us understand the explosion of "fake news" and wild far-right conspiracy theories. More generally, the destabilization of those sectors of the working class that had previously enjoyed some stability but have since been abandoned by capital and the precarious condition that a majority of workers now share, especially young workers, as I discussed in the previous chapter, is a powerful structural shift brought about capitalist globalization and crisis that exercises a newfound *centripetal* pull on working-class unity that cuts across racial, ethnic, and national divisions. However, the *centrifugal* forces militating against that unity are numerous, including racist and national chauvinist manipulation from above of fear and insecurity, the relative absence of a socialist left that could provide an alternative appeal, and liberal identitarian politics that eschews the language of class and the critique of capital.

The United States provides a case study in these contradictory dynamics. The conditions of unemployment, deteriorating living standards, and social decay generate anger and despair and have helped fuel fascist politics. It is telling that in the areas abandoned by capitalist investment, especially the agricultural breadbaskets and the deindustrialized Rust Belt of the Midwest, many counties switched from Obama in 2012 to Trump in 2016, as the Democrats relentlessly pursued neoliberal policies at home and wars abroad, with the result that despair and immiseration spread and social polarization escalated. It is similarly unsurprising that the presidential campaigns of both Bernie Sanders and Donald Trump in the 2016 presidential election, the one with a left interpretation of the crisis and the other with a far-right populist and openly racist interpretation, won broad support among disaffected workers who later came to embrace Trumpism.[54] In October 2020, the government broke up a conspiracy by the far-right militia organization the Wolverine Watchmen to kidnap and possibly kill the governor of the US state of Michigan. It is revealing that the leader of the plot, Adam Fox, a poor white man, lost his job during the pandemic yet was not eligible for unemployment benefits and received no public assistance, even as trillions went to bail out the banks and corporations. Thrust into destitution, he lost his dwelling and was forced to move into the basement of a friend's house.[55] The majority of those who stormed the US Capitol building three months later faced serious financial troubles, including bankruptcies, notices of eviction or foreclosure, precarious employment, and mounting debt.[56]

Both of the parties that rotate in and out of power in the United States offer nothing more than more hardship and abandonment to these sectors of the working class. It is these conditions of despair and contempt for the political and economic elite that make the mass of working-class whites in the United States so susceptible to the fascist appeal. The appeal expresses in distorted form this despair and contempt, and although it offers false promises and illusory solutions it touches a raw nerve among these sectors by acknowledging

and validating their fear and despair. Yet neither does the identitarian "left" offer anything to these sectors. To the contrary,
they are written off and maligned as racists who are simply
lashing out to defend their "white privilege" or, in the now
infamous words of the 2016 Democratic candidate for the
presidency Hillary Clinton, as "baskets of deplorables." The
anomie and nihilism of capitalist culture adds a rich fertilizer
to the mix. In the larger picture, the global social order generates all kinds of pathologies, but the identitarian "left" also
ends up providing oxygen to the far-right and fascist appeal.
It encourages these sectors to identify as whites with their
own white identity interests rather than as workers, and, thus,
ends up stoking the white nationalism that has swept through
the ranks of these sectors and made them more susceptible to
the appeal. The problem here, as a matter of course, is not a
struggle against racism, for that must be front and center of
any emancipatory project, rather, it is the separation of race
from class, the substitution of politics based on essentialized
identities for politics based on the working class, with everyone belonging to one or another identity group, and with all
members of the group assumed to share the same interests.
Yet the only chance that popular resistance forces have to beat
back the threat of fascism is to put forward an alternative
interpretation of the crisis based on working-class politics that
can win over the would-be social base of fascism.

Fascist projects can only forge a social base at the expense
of the repressive super-exploitation and/or exclusion of sectors
of the population. Ideologically, these sectors are turned into
"Others," so that social anxiety is externally sublimated. "The
loss of privileges or their threatened loss will not necessarily
provide a spontaneous abandonment of opportunism
within the upper strata of the working class," wrote Lenin,
in discussing what he termed the labor aristocracy, "On the
contrary, it can fuel a powerful reaction within these sectors
to 'blame' the workers in the lower strata or in other counties

for the loss or threatened loss of these privileges."[57] But this "powerful reaction" is not automatic. Key to it is a particular interpretation of the crisis put forth by organic intellectuals of both liberalism and neofascism that exteriorizes the internal contradictions of capitalism in crisis and by fascist organizers that exteriorize these contradictions onto subordinate racial, ethnic, or national groups. While some right-wing populist and neofascist movements in Europe do promise a restoration of the social contract between the state and the working class, this promise is founded on a racist xenophobia and nationalism that excludes large swaths of the population cast out as "Others." Moreover, it is difficult to see how much of the TCC would support a project that proposes a withdrawal from globalization processes and a material rather than a mere psychological wage of fascism, as these would undermine the prerogatives of transnational accumulation.

Authoritarian state power and a fascist mobilization in civil society will not, in my view, be enough to bring about full-blown fascist systems. This is because fascism involves a *triangulation* of reactionary and repressive power in the state (including the state's armed bodies) and a fascist mobilization in civil society *with predatory transnational capital*. For the moment, it appears that the major portion of the TCC is not prepared to support fascist projects. In the United States, for instance, the TCC was delighted with Trump's economic policies—deregulation, privatizations, anti-worker measures, regressive tax reform, and so on, but the corporate elite and their leading business association came out firmly against Trump's effort to steal the 2020 elections in what amounted to an attempted coup d'état. In Europe, much of the TCC campaigned against BREXIT and has pushed back against far-right and neofascist parties that call for rolling back globalization. I have long argued that, far from being monolithic, any real internal unity of the global ruling class is impossible. The TCC is wracked by fierce competition, conflicting pressures, and differences over the tactics and strategy of maintaining class domination and addressing the crises and contradictions of global capitalism. But it *is* united in its shared interest in an open global economy and in suppressing challenges to its rule from below. Mounting crises of state legitimacy have heightened the splits and infighting within the ruling groups (in part, the strongmen and fascists have won popularity because their populist discourse has resonated with masses of people in the face of the legitimacy crisis). Should the global revolt reach a point where it comes to threaten the very rule of capital, the TCC may be more willing to turn to fascism to maintain control.

Yet, short of fascism, the TCC has already turned to extending the global police. Savage global inequalities are politically explosive, and to the extent that the system is simply unable to reverse them it turns to ever more violent forms of containment to manage immiserated populations as balance between consent and coercion shifts toward the latter. As I discussed at length in my earlier study *The Global Police State*, well before the pandemic, the agents of the emerging global police state had been developing new modalities of state-organized violence, warfare, and social control made possible by applications of digitalization and fourth industrial revolution technologies examined in chapter two. These include artificial intelligence–powered autonomous weaponry, such as unmanned attack and transportation vehicles, robot soldiers, a new generation of superdrones and flybots, hypersonic weapons, microwave guns that immobilize, cyberattack and information warfare, biometric identification, state data mining, and global electronic surveillance that allows for eavesdropping on virtually all communications and the tracking and control of every movement. State data mining and global electronic surveillance are now expanding the theater of conflict from active war zones to militarized cities and rural localities around the world, as data and surveillance become totalizing. These combine with a restructuring of space that allows for new forms of spatial containment and control of the marginalized. In fact, by 2018, there were no less than sixty-three physical walls built by states worldwide to keep in or lock out unwanted or rebellious populations.[58]

We saw in chapter one that the pandemic allowed ruling groups to ratchet up the global police state, indeed, how they utilized the health emergency to achieve a greater level of police state normalization. The global police state has been centrally aimed at the coercive exclusion of surplus humanity, who are disproportionately drawn from the racially oppressed, the ethnically persecuted, religious and national minorities, migrants and refugees, and other vulnerable communities. But its ultimate target is the global working class in its entirety, especially as the new round of digitally driven restructuring throws ever more people into the ranks of the surplus labor and the precariat. The result is permanent low-intensity warfare meant to disarticulate popular insurgency from below. The TCC and its state agents are acutely aware that humanity is now entering a state of de facto civil war. "The convergence of more information and more people with fewer state resources will constrain governments' efforts to address rampant poverty, violence, and pollution, and create a breeding ground for dissatisfaction among increasingly aware, yet still disempowered populations," stated a 2019 US Army report. "A global populace that is increasingly attuned and sensitive to disparities in economic resources and the diffusion of social influence will lead to further challenges to the status quo and lead to system rattling events." These "system rattling events," include "the Arab Spring, the Color Revolutions of Eastern Europe, the Greek monetary crisis, BREXIT, and the mass migrations to Europe from the Middle East and North Africa."[59] A year earlier, a Pentagon war game envisioned a "Zbellion" that would take place in the year 2025." According to the imagined scenario, a cadre of disaffected "Zoomers" launch a protest movement in the United States that begins in "parks, rallies, protests, and coffee shops" and also involves a "global cyber campaign to expose injustice and corruption and to support causes it deem[s] beneficial," as the rebellion spreads to Europe and cities throughout the world.[60]

THE END OF THE BEGINNING OR THE BEGINNING OF THE END?

In chapter one, I identified three types of crisis: cyclical, structural, and systemic. Recall that structural crises are so-called because their resolution requires restructuring the system, whereas a systemic crisis implies that its resolution must involve a supersession of the existing socioeconomic system, in this case capitalism. Historically crises resolve the tensions and contradictions that build up in the capitalist economy. They lead to a new surge of centralization and concentration of capital as it depreciates, as firms merge, go out of business, or are snatched up by bigger firms, as stockpiles are exhausted, and as the total wage bill declines. New technologies and forms of organization may spur investment and growth that restore the accumulation process and pave the way for a new wave of chaotic expansion. *Resolve* in these cases means *displacement*, either in *time*, so that the contradictions reappear in the future, often more acutely than before, or in *space*, to more vulnerable countries, regions, and peoples in the world capitalist system.

Globalization, however, has so integrated all countries and regions of the world that spatial containment of crises may now be impossible. To date, capitalism, as a global system, has proved remarkably resilient, even as it has faced one crisis after another in its centuries-long existence, defying predictions of its imminent demise and emerging renewed after each major crisis. It would be foolish to assume we are in the end game of global capitalism. The new round of digitally driven restructuring discussed in chapter two, combined with an intensification of militarized accumulation and accumulation by repression, may turbocharge the economy enough to usher in a period of rising profits and prosperity for the system as a whole, even as millions—or billions—sink into greater precariousness and desolation.

Economic restructuring through digitalization, in my view, may restore accumulation in the short run, but for the system to survive there must be social and political changes of a far-reaching nature. These changes are even less predictable than our analyses of the economy, because, as I have stressed throughout this study, they are highly contingent on how struggles among social and class forces play out around the world. Even if deficit spending and Keynesian stimulus that expanded during the pandemic remain in place, as I noted in chapter one, the experience of the financial collapse of 2008 showed that governments recovered the costs of bailouts by deepening social austerity, even as banks and corporations used bailout money to buy back stock and engage in new rounds of predatory activities.

On the other hand, it is during moments not of equilibrium but of crisis that the intervention of agency can be most effective in bringing about structural change. Crises are key conjunctures when significant structural—and, in rare historic moments, systemic—change becomes possible. Short of revolution, the popular classes must struggle now to prevent the ruling groups from turning the crisis into an opportunity for them to resuscitate and deepen the neoliberal order once the dust settles. Their struggle is to push for something along the lines of a global Green New Deal as an interim program alongside an accumulation of forces for more radical system change.[1] A Green New Deal, a call first put out in the United States, proposes combining sweeping green policies, including an end to fossil fuels, with a social welfare and pro-worker economy that would include mass employment opportunities in green energy and other technologies. A global Green New Deal may help lift the world out of economic depression as it simultaneously addresses the climate emergency and generates favorable conditions to struggle for a post-capitalist social order.

While the ruling groups deploy the new digital technologies to enhance their control and profit-making, this same technical infrastructure of the fourth industrial revolution is producing the resources from which a political and economic system very different from the global capitalism in which we live could be achieved. As many have noted, these technologies could be used to free us from the drudgeries of menial and dull work, drastically reducing socially necessary labor time and increasing leisure time.[2] They may allow us to overcome obstacles that socialist-oriented economic planning in the twentieth century experienced once the price (market) mechanism of coordinating capitalist production had been suppressed. Under an entirely different social and economic system we human beings could cease being slaves to machines and technologies employed for the purpose of exploitation and instead become masters of them. In an inversion of Marx's observation that living labor is dominated by dead labor, we living human beings could wield the collective power of all those who came before us, that is, the fruits of thousands of years of collective human labor and ingenuity, to unleash our human potential and emancipate ourselves. If we are to free ourselves through these new technologies, however, we must first overthrow the oppressive and antediluvian social relations of global capitalism.

What does the future hold? As the global civil war heats up in the post-pandemic world there will be societal disinte-gration and political collapse. We have seen that the pandemic and its aftermath served as a hothouse accelerating the crisis of capitalist rule more that anyone could have predicted. The crisis generates enormous political tensions that must be managed by the ruling groups. It animates geopolitical conflict, as states seek to externalize social and political tensions, and accelerates the breakdown of the post–World War II international order, increasing the danger of international military conflagration. The poor and dispossessed will continue to rise up in countless struggles. We are clearly facing a revolutionary situation as described by Lenin, in which the prevailing system is in crisis, the suffering of the oppressed has grown more acute, and the masses are stepping up their historic action.

In the absence of a clear program that targets the system or a left that could help channel uprisings against the underlying causes of distress and deprivation, we are likely to see desperation erupt into racial, ethnic, religious, and other forms of aggression and into social violence among the oppressed themselves. There is no such thing as "senseless violence," insofar as we are always able to make sense of it through analysis of its causes. Fueled by the anomie and nihilism of global capitalist culture and a gangster capitalism from above, people whose very existence is at risk will develop survival strategies that may put them in a position to be criminalized by a capitalist state that remits the crimes of the rich and the powerful, while harshly punishing those of the poor. We are precisely in the situation described by Gramsci that so many people have of late cited, and with good reason: "The crisis consists precisely in the fact that the old way is dying and the new cannot be born; in this interregnum a great variety of morbid symptoms appear."[3] At this time, we are unequivocally at the interregnum. The failure to either radically reform global capitalism or to replace it with a democratic socialism raises the specter of barbarism, as Gramsci's contemporary Rosa Luxemburg prophetically warned, or of a collapse of global civilization, hastened on by the climate emergency and looming ecological holocaust.

I am not pessimistic. Despite the sobering discussion above on the challenges that emancipatory projects face, the crisis of ruling class hegemony opens up enormous prospects for a viable counterhegemony. Capitalist crises may originate at the deepest level as a structural contradiction, but they are played out in the terrain of politics, culture, and ideology. A counterhegemony depends in part on how the crisis is understood and interpreted by masses of people, which in turn depends, in significant part, on a *systemic* critique of global capitalism and on organic intellectuals in the Gramscian sense, intellectuals who attach themselves to and serve the emancipatory struggles of the popular classes, and who are committed to putting forth such a critique. It has been my aim in this study to contribute, however modestly, to such a critique.

NOTES

Introduction

1   See Alex Ferrer, Terra Graziani, and Jacob Woocher, "Nearly 1,000 Homeless People Died in LA in 2020 as 93,000 Homes Sit Vacant," *Truthout*, October, 23 2020, accessed October 14, 2021, https://truthout.org/articles/nearly-1000-homeless-people-died-in-la-in-2020-as-93000-homes-sit-vacant.

2   See Elizabeth Chou, "Families Occupying Caltrans-Owned Homes in El Sereno Forcibly Removed by CHP," *Los Angeles Daily News*, November 27, 2020, accessed on October, 14 2021, https://tinyurl.com/36zmsrum.

3   William I. Robinson, *A Theory of Global Capitalism* (Baltimore: Johns Hopkins University Press, 2004); William I. Robinson, *Global Capitalism and the Crisis of Humanity* (New York: Cambridge University Press, 2014); William I. Robinson, *The Global Police State* (London: Pluto, 2020). I also published two lengthy case studies that applied my theory of global capitalism: William I. Robinson, *Transnational Conflicts: Central America, Social Change, and Globalization* (London: Verso, 2003); William I. Robinson, *Latin America and Global Capitalism* (Baltimore: Johns Hopkins University Press, 2008).

Chapter 1

1   Bank of America, "Covid-19 Investment Implications Series: The World after Covid Primer," May 5, 2020, accessed on 8 November 2020, unavailable October 14, 2021, https://www.bofaml.com/content/dam/boamlimages/documents/articles/ID20_0467/the_world_after_covid.pdf.

2   Jack Rasmus, "Does Worldwide Economic Depression Lie Ahead?" in Cynthia McKinney, ed., *When China Sneezes: From the Coronavirus Lockdown to the Global Politico-Economic Implications* (Atlanta: Clarity Press, 2020).

3   World Bank, *Global Economic Prospects* (Washington, DC: World Bank, June 2020), xiii. The Bank estimated a year-end drop of 7 percent in the United States, 6.1 percent in the euro area, 9.1 percent in Japan, 7.2 percent for Latin America and the Caribbean, 4.2 percent for the Middle East and North Africa, 2.7 percent for South Asia, and 2.8 for sub-Saharan Africa. Moreover, growth in China nearly ground to a halt (the Bank estimated 1 percent growth), meaning that unlike 2008, growth in China (and other "emerging markets") would not establish a floor for the decline in the rest of the world (table 1.1, p. 4). The US economy shrank by an annual rate of 33 percent in the second quarter of 2020, the single worst GDP slump in US history; see Carmen Reinicke, "US GDP Plunged by a Record 33% Annual Rate in the 2nd Quarter as Coronavirus Lockdowns Raged," Business Insider, July 30, 2020, accessed on October 14, 2021, https://tinyurl.com/yjw8tyr7. The data Reinicke cites is from the US Commerce Department.

4   Cited in Joseph Choonara, *Unravelling Capitalism* (London: Bookmarks Publications, 2009), 66.

5   Karl Marx, "Wage Labor and Capital," in Robert C. Tucker, ed., *The Marx-Engels Reader* (New York: W.W. Norton, 1978), 214.

6   Joseph Choona, *Unravelling Capitalism* (London: Bookmarks, 2009), 120; citing data from the *Financial Times*.

7   See, inter alia, Ronald W. Cox, "The Crisis of Capitalism through Global Value Chains," *Class, Race and Corporate Power*, 7, no. 1 (2019); Eric Toussaint, "No, the Coronavirus Is Not Responsible for the Fall in Stock Prices," *Monthly Review*, March 4, 2020, accessed October 14, 2021, https://mronline.org/2020/03/04/no-the-coronavirus-is-not-responsible-for-the-fall-of-stock-prices.

8   "The Problem with Profits," *Economist*, May 26, 2016, accessed October 14, 2021, https://www.economist.com/leaders/2016/03/26/the-problem-with-profits.

9   "Hanging Together, *Economist*, May 16, 2020, 60, accessed October 14, 2021, https://www.economist.com/news/2013/11/18/hanging-together.

10   See William I. Robinson: *Promoting Polyarchy: Globalization, U.S. Intervention, and Hegemony* (New York: Cambridge University Press, 1996); William I. Robinson, *Latin America and Global Capitalism* (Baltimore: Johns Hopkins University Press, 2008).

11   For my latest summary iteration on the TCC, see William I. Robinson, *The Global Police State* (London: Pluto Press, 2020). For a concise summary of the development of this concept and a review of the scholarship, see William I. Robinson and Jeb Sprague, "The Transnational Capitalist Class," in Mark Juergensmeyer, Saskia

Sassen, and Manfred Steger, eds., *Oxford Handbook of Global Studies* (New York: Oxford University Press, 2018).

12   On the TCC and the new global economy, see in particular William I. Robinson, *A Theory of Global Capitalism* (Baltimore: Johns Hopkins University Press, 2004); William I. Robinson, *Global Capitalism and the Crisis of Humanity* (New York: Cambridge University Press, 2014).

13   Singaporean academic Kishore Mahbubani noted in 2010, a decade before the outbreak: "The seven billion people who inhabit the planet earth no longer live in more than one hundred separate boats [countries]. Instead, they all live in 193 separate cabins on the same boat. If we are stuck together on a virus-infected ship, does it make sense to clean and scrub only our personal cabins while ignoring the corridors and air wells outside through which the virus travels? The answer is clearly no"; cited in Klaus Schwab and Thierry Malleret, *Covid-19: The Great Reset* (Geneva: Forum Publishing, 2020), 22.

14   "Wealth: Having It All and Wanting More," Oxfam: Policy and Practice, January 19, 2015, accessed October 14, 2021, http://policy-practice. oxfam.org.uk/publications/wealth-having-it-all-and-wanting-more-338125.

15   "To the possessor of money capital the process of production appears merely as an unavoidable intermediate link, as a necessary evil for the sake of money-making. All nations with a capitalist mode of production are therefore seized periodically by a feverish attempt to make money without the intervention of the process of production"; Karl Marx, *Capital*, vol. 2 (Moscow: Progress Publishers, 1971 [1893]), 58.

16   General Accounting Office (GAO), "Federal Reserve System: Opportunities Exist to Strengthen Policies and Processes for Managing Emergency Assistance," July 2011, accessed October 18, 2021, https://www.gao.gov/products/gao-11-696.

17   On fictitious capital and more generally on the financialization, see, inter alia, Cedric Durand, *Fictitious Capital: How Finance Is Appropriating Our Future* (London: Verso, 2017).

18   J.B. Maverick, "How Big Is the Derivatives Market," Investopedia, January 22, 2018, accessed October 14, 2021, https://www. investopedia.com/ask/answers/052715/how-big-derivatives-market.asp. On total global debt, see Andrea Shalal, "Global Debt Reaches Record High of 331% of GDP in First Quarter: IIF," Reuters, July 16, 2020, accessed October 14, 2021, https://tinyurl.com/5a2y3xp6.

19   Shalal, "Global Debt Reaches Record High of 331% of GDP in First Quarter: IIF."

20 Paul Wiseman, Bernard Condon, and Cathy Bussewitz, AP News, "Corporate Debt Loads a Rising Risk as Virus Hits Economy," March 11, 2020, accessed October 14, 2021, https://apnews.com/7cd0108d 79c6b4f1ee2e6ec5fc3a2275.

21 See William I. Robinson, "Global Capitalist Crisis and Trump's War Drive," Truthout, April 19, 2017, accessed October 14, 2021, http:// www.truth-out.org/opinion/item/40266-global-capitalist-crisis-and-trump-s-war-drive; "Global Homeland Security and Public Safety Market Report 2019—Market Is Expected to Grow from $431 Billion in 2018 to $606 Billion in 2024," CISION PR Newswire, February 6, 2019, accessed October 14, 2021, https://tinyurl.com/ ejucmprn.

22 Aude Fleurant, Alexandra Kuimova, Nan Tian, Pieter D. Wezeman, and Seimon T. Wezeman, "The SIPRI Top 100 Arms-Producing and Military Services Companies, 2016," Stockholm International Peace Research Institute (SIPRI), December 2017, accessed October 14, 2021, https://www.sipri.org/sites/default/files/2017-12/fs_arms_ industry_2016.pdf.

23 William Langewiesche, "The Chaos Company," *Vanity Fair*, April 2004, accessed October 14, 2021, https://archive.vanityfair.com/ article/2014/4/the-chaos-company.

24 Niall McCarthy, "Private Security Outnumbers the Police in Most Countries Worldwide," *Forbes*, August 31, 2017, accessed October 14, 2021, https://tinyurl.com/4ru5ucb7.

25 For extended discussion, see various chapters in Cynthia McKinney, ed., *When China Sneezes: From the Coronavirus Lockdown to the Global Politico-Economic Implications* (Atlanta: Clarity Press, 2020). The US government does not deny that the Defense Advanced Research Projects Agency (DARPA) and several other agencies conduct bioweapon research. In 2017, the US government lifted its ban on gain of function research; also see Kees van der Pijl, "Health Emergency or Seizure of Power? The political Economy of COVID-19," New Cold War, April 27, 2020, accessed October 14, 2021, https:// www.newcoldwar.org/health-emergency-or-seizure-of-power-the-political-economy-of-covid-19, and the numerous sources he references. It should be noted that the US bioweapons program far outstrips those of other countries; see van der Pijl for the figure of Pentagon labs in twenty-five countries.

26 "French Nobel Prize Winner: 'Covid-19 Made in Lab,'" Connexion, March 3, 2021, accessed October 14, 2021, https://tinyurl.com/ u6eb68.

27 Cited in Laurie Garrett, "Biology's Brave New World: The Promise and Perils of the Synbio Revolution," in *The Fourth Industrial*

Revolution: A Davos Reader (Washington, DC: Council on Foreign Affairs, 2016), 68.

28   Van der Pijl, "Health Emergency or Seizure of Power?"

29   See Daniel C. Hellinger, *Conspiracies and Conspiracy Theory in the Age of Trump* (London: Palgrave Macmillan, 2019).

30   More recently there are also absurd conspiracy theories that spread on social media in which people simply hear wild claims and believe them in the context of what are often right-wing agendas, in what Rosenblum and Muirhead refer to as "the new conspiracism"; Nancy L. Rosenblum and Russell Muirhead, *A Lot of People are Saying: The New Conspiracism and the Assault on Democracy* (Princeton, NJ: Princeton University Press, 2020). On a related note, Timothy Erik Strom has pointed out that some conspiratorial thinking with regard to vaccines and medicine has been grounded in legitimate critique: "Distrust in scientific medicine increased across the 1970s.... Much of this drew on the very real abuse of research subjects, the mass marketing of dubious drugs, an increasing awareness of ecological degradation and toxification, the medicalization of childbirth, and the corruption of GPs and university researchers by corporate powers"; Timothy Erik Ström, "Antennas Aflame: Cybernetics, Conspiracies, and 5G," *Arena Quarterly* no. 4, December 2020, accessed October 14, 2021, https://arena.org.au/antennas-aflame-cybernetics-conspiracies-and-5g.

31   See Steven Lee Myers, "China Spins Tale That the U.S. Army Started the Coronavirus," *New York Times*, March 13, 2020, accessed October 14, 2021, https://www.nytimes.com/2020/03/13/world/asia/coronavirus-china-conspiracy-theory.html.

32   Jeff J. Brown, "Everything You Wanted to Know About Coronaviruses," in McKinney, *When China Sneezes*; the figures for the vaccine market are on p. 28.

33   The two companies that stand out are Inovio Pharmaceuticals and Moderna; see inter alia, Paul Sonne, "How a Secretive Pentagon Agency Seeded the Ground for a Rapid Coronavirus Cure," *Washington Post*, July 30, 2020, accessed October 14, 2021, https://tinyurl.com/ufwka9mz; Witnew Webb, "Bats, Gene Editing and Bioweapons: Recent DARPA Experiments Raise Concerns amid Coronavirus Outbreak," in McKinney, *When China Sneezes*.

34   On the Gates Foundation agenda, see Vandanna Shiva, et al., *Gates to a Global Empire: Over Seed, Food, Health, Knowledge … and the Earth* (Florence, IT: Navdanya International, 2020), accessed October 14, 2021, https://navdanyainternational.org/publications/gates-to-a-global-empire; also see Mark Curtis, *Gated Development: Is the Gates Foundation Always a Force for Good?* (London: Global Justice Now, 2016),

accessed October 14, 2021, https://www.globaljustice.org.uk/sites/default/files/gated_development_final_version.pdf; Jan Urhalın, "Bill Gate's Foundation Is Leading a Green Counterrevolution in Africa," *Jacobin*, December 27, 2020, accessed October 14, 2021, https://tinyurl.com/z9f934z5.

35   Cited in Strom, "Antennas Aflame," 6.

36   See, inter alia, Jenni Spinner, "Gates Foundation Enlists Novartis, GSK, Others in COVID-19 Fight," Outsourcing-Pharma, March 27, 2020, accessed October 14, 2021, https://tinyurl.com/svdswe8; KP Narayana Kumar, "Controversial Vaccine Studies: Why Is Bill and Melinda Gates Foundation Under Fire from Critics in India?" *Economic Times*, August 31, 2014, accessed October 14, 2021, https://tinyurl.com/3z3p845a.

37   Van der Pijl, "Health Emergency or Seizure of Power?"

38   Helen Buyniski, "The Post-COVID-19 World: A Permanent Dystopia?" in McKinney, *When China Sneezes*, 291.

39   Ibid.

40   On public sourcing versus corporate control of vaccines, see Alexander Zaitchik, "How to Break a Big Pharma Monopoly on a COVID-19 Vaccine," *New Republic*, August 24, 2020, accessed October 14, 2021, https://newrepublic.com/article/159019/break-big-pharma-monopoly-covid-19-vaccine; Amnesty International, "Wealthy Countries Already Hoarding Breakthrough Vaccines" (press release), November 9, 2020, accessed October 14, 2021, https://www.amnesty.org/en/latest/news/2020/11/wealthy-countries-already-hoarding-breakthrough-vaccines. A group of international social justice organizations that included Amnesty International, Oxfam, Global Justice Now, and Frontline AIDS formed the People's Vaccine Alliance, which charged that a handful of rich countries were hoarding vaccines and undermining access by poor countries; see Amnesty International, "Campaigners Warn That 9 out of 10 People in Poor Countries Are Set to Miss Out on COVID-19 Vaccine Next Year," December 9, 2020, accessed October 14, 2021, https://tinyurl.com/tenvyf4.

41   See, e.g., van der Pijl, "Health Emergency or Seizure of Power?"; Piers Robinson, "The Propaganda of Terror and Fear: A Lesson from Recent History," *Guardian*, March 28, 2020, accessed October 14, 2021, https://off-guardian.org/2020/03/28/the-propaganda-of-terror-and-fear-a-lesson-from-recent-history.

42   Van der Pijl, "Health Emergency or Seizure of Power?"

43   *Scenarios for the Future of Technology and International Development* (Albany, NY: Rockefeller Institute/Global Business Network, 2010),

19, accessed on October 14, 2021, http://www.nommeraadio.ee/meedia/pdf/RRS/Rockefeller%20Foundation.pdf.

44   See Event 201, accessed October 14, 2021, https://www.centerforhealthsecurity.org/event201/about; also see Event 201, "Public-Private Cooperation for Pandemic Preparedness and Response," accessed October 14, 2021, https://www.centerforhealthsecurity.org/event201/recommendations.html.

45   Robinson, "The Propaganda of Terror and Fear."

46   In the United States, the mass media, the mainstream, and the left fell into a reification with regard to documented racial disparities in coronavirus deaths that would be comical if it weren't a topic of such tragedy. The racial disparities in the impact of coronavirus, of course, are accounted for by the racial disparities in access to adequate health care, diet, and housing, as well as hazardous employment and so on. In other words, "race" was a proxy for these conditions. Studies showed that once class was factored in (itself measured by proxy as an income category), it was socioeconomic conditions that determined the likelihood of death; see, inter alia, the excellent article by Walter Benn Michaels and Adolph Reed, Jr., "The Trouble with Disparity," Nonsite.org, September 10, 2020, accessed October 14, 2021, https://nonsite.org/the-trouble-with-disparity. Race, as we know, is a fictitious category of nineteenth-century pseudoscience that cannot "cause" anything whatsoever. But this did not stop the popularization of a narrative in which some genetic or biological factor attributed to "race" was purported to explain the disproportionate impact of the disease. In one broadcast, CNN's chief medical correspondent would declare in all seriousness that there are "biological factors" associated with "being a person of color—Black, Latino Latinx or Native American" that cause the disparity; see Michaels and Reed, Jr., "The Trouble with Disparity," 7.

47   FAO, IFAD, UNICEF, WFP and WHO, *The State of Food Security and Nutrition in the World: Transforming Food Systems for Affordable Healthy Diets* (Rome: FAO, 2020), xvi, 3, accessed October 14, 2021, https://reliefweb.int/sites/reliefweb.int/files/resources/SOFI2020_EN_web.pdf.

48   "Half a Billion People Could be Pushed into Poverty by Coronavirus, Warns Oxfam" (press release), Oxfam International, April 9, 2020, accessed October 14, 2021, https://www.oxfam.org/en/press-releases/half-billion-people-could-be-pushed-poverty-coronavirus-warns-oxfam.

49   "COVID-19 and Europe's Environment: Impacts of a Global Pandemic," European Environmental Agency, November 5, 2020,

updated March 25, 2021, accessed October 14, 2021, https://www.
eea.europa.eu/publications/covid-19-and-europe-s.

50 In particular, see Rob Wallace, *Big Farms Make Big Flu: Dispatches on Influenza, Agribusiness, and the Nature of Science* (New York: Monthly Review Press, 2016).

51 Ibid.

52 "COVID-19 and Europe's Environment."

53 Schwab and Malleret, *Covid-19: The Great Reset*, 138.

54 "Remarks by President Trump, Vice President Pence, and Members of the Coronavirus Task Force in Press Conference," White House Archive, March 13, 2020, accessed October 14, 2021 https://tinyurl.com/kp8utyzy.

55 "Covid-19 Investment Implications Series."

56 See, e.g., "How Major Economies Are Trying to Mitigate the Coronavirus Shock," *Financial Times*, March 30, 2020, accessed October 14, 2021, https://www.ft.com/content/26af5520-6793-11ea-800d-da70cff6e4d3.

57 "China Signals Ramped-Up Stimulus as Coronavirus Impact Widens," Bloomberg, March 27, 2020, accessed October 14, 2021, https://www.bloomberg.com/news/articles/2020-03-27/china-pledges-to-raise-fiscal-deficit-ratio-sell-special-debt.

58 "Corporate Bail-Outs: Bottomless Pit, Inc.," *Economist*, April 4, 2020, 8, accessed October 14, 2021, https://www.economist.com/leaders/2020/04/04/bail-outs-are-inevitable-and-toxic.

59 The most comprehensive country-by-country summary was provided by the International Monetary Fund, "Policy Responses to COVID-19," accessed October 14, 2021, https://www.imf.org/en/Topics/imf-and-covid19/Policy-Responses-to-COVID-19.

60 "2.7 Billion People Have Had No Social Protection to Cope with Covid-19 Economic Crisis" (press release), Oxfam International, December 15, 2020, accessed October 14, 2021, https://tinyurl.com/swrv7k54.

61 "Billionaires: Since Pandemic Began U.S. Billionaires' Net Worths [*sic*] Jump $931 Billion, Or Nearly One-Third, as Working Families Suffer," Americans for Tax Fairness/Institute for Policy Studies, October 20, 2020, accessed October 14, 2021, https://tinyurl.com/xkhhstce.

62 Rupert Neate, "Billionaires' Wealth Rises to $10.2 Trillion amid Covid Crisis," *Guardian*, October 6, 2020, accessed October 14, 2021, https://www.theguardian.com/business/2020/oct/07/covid-19-crisis-boosts-the-fortunes-of-worlds-billionaires.

63 For extended discussion of the increasingly gangster character of global capitalism, see Michael Woodiwiss, *Gangster Capitalism: The*

United States and the Global Rise of Organized Crime (New York: Carol and Graf Publishers, 2005).

64   Tom Warren et al., "Billions in Dirty Money Rolled through Deutsche Bank," BuzzFeed News, September 20, 2020, accessed October 14, 2021, https://www.buzzfeednews.com/article/tomwarren/deutsche-bank-money-laundering-mirror-trades.

65   *Fleecing Patients: Hospitals Charge Patients More Than Four Times the Cost of Care* (Oakland: National Nurses United, 2020), accessed October 14, 2021, https://act.nationalnursesunited.org/page/-/files/graphics/1120_CostChargeRatios_Report_FINAL_PP.pdf.

66   "Almost 25 Million Jobs Could Be Lost Worldwide as a Result of COVID-19" (press release), International Labour Organization, March 18, 2020, accessed October 14, 2021, https://www.ilo.org/global/about-the-ilo/newsroom/news/WCMS_738742/lang--en/index.htm.

67   "ILO: As Job Losses Escalate, Nearly Half of Global Workforce at Risk of Losing Livelihoods" (press release), International Labour Organization, April 29, 2020, accessed October 14, 2021, https://www.ilo.org/global/about-the-ilo/newsroom/news/WCMS_743036/lang--en/index.htm.

68   "ILO: 34 Million Jobs Lost by the COVID-19 Crisis in Latin America and the Caribbean" (press release), International Labour Organization, October 1, 2020, accessed October 14, 2021, http://www.ilo.org/global/about-the-ilo/newsroom/news/WCMS_756771/lang--en/index.htm.

69   Alexander Weber, "Global Crisis Damage from Covid-19 Is Now About 255 Million Jobs," Bloomberg, January 25, 2021, accessed October 14, 2021, https://tinyurl.com/k9df5hfv.

70   "The 90% Economy," *Economist*, April 30, 2020, 7, accessed October 14, 2021, https://www.economist.com/weeklyedition/2020-05-02.

71   My most complete exposition of the concept of transnational state apparatuses is Robinson, *Global Capitalism and the Crisis of Humanity*, chapter two, "Notes on Transnational State Apparatuses."

72   Cited in Phil Hearse and Neil Faulkner, "The Coming Social Collapse," Mutiny, April 2020, accessed October 15, 2021, https://www.timetomutiny.org/post/the-coming-social-collapse.

73   See, inter alia, "The IMF's Response to COVID-19," International Monetary Fund, October 28, 2020, updated April 8, 2021, accessed October 15, 2021, https://www.imf.org/en/About/FAQ/imf-response-to-covid-19#Q1; G20: Italia 2021, accessed October 15, 2021, https://tinyurl.com/3cz4358f.

74   "Covid-19 Investment Implications Series."

75   "Global: 140 Countries Pass Counterterror Laws Since 9/11," Human
     Rights Watch, June 29, 2012, accessed October 15, 2021, https://www.
     hrw.org/news/2012/06/29/global-140-countries-pass-counterterror-
     laws-9/11.

76   Natasha Singer and Choe Sang-Hun, "As Coronavirus Surveillance
     Escalates, Personal Privacy Plummets," *New York Times*, April 17, 2020,
     accessed October 15, 2021, https://www.nytimes.com/2020/03/23/
     technology/coronavirus-surveillance-tracking-privacy.html.

77   See, inter alia, "No Vaccine for Cruelty," *Economist*, October 17, 2020,
     50–52.

78   Maria R. Sahuquillo, Silvia Blanco, and Macarena Vidal Liy,
     "Democracia en Cuarentena por Coronavirus," *El Pais* (Spain), March 30,
     2020, accessed October 15, 2021, https://elpais.com/internacional/
     2020-03-30/democracia-en-cuarentena-por-coronavirus.html.

79   "Armies Are Mobilizing against the Coronavirus," *Economist*,
     March 23, 2020, accessed October 15, 2021, https://www.
     economist.com/international/2020/03/23/armies-are-mobilising-
     against-the-coronavirus.

80   Shaun Walker and Jennifer Rankin, "Hungary Passes Law That Will Let
     Orban Rule by Decree," *Guardian*, March 30, 2020, accessed October
     15, 2021, https://www.theguardian.com/world/2020/mar/30/
     hungary-jail-for-coronavirus-misinformation-viktor-orban.

81   Paul Hockenos, "Coronavirus and the Dawn of Post-Democratic
     Europe," *Foreign Policy*, March 31, 2020, accessed October 15,
     2021, https://foreignpolicy.com/2020/03/31/hungary-orban-
     coronavirus-europe-democracy.

82   Selam Gebrekidan, "For Autocrats, Coronavirus Is a Chance to Grab
     Even More Power," *New York Times*, March 30, 2020, accessed October
     15, 2021, https://www.nytimes.com/2020/03/30/world/europe/
     coronavirus-governments-power.html.

83   Peter Wade, "DOJ Wants to Suspend Certain Constitutional
     Rights during Coronavirus Emergency," *Rolling Stone*, March
     21, 2020, accessed October 15, 2021, https://www.rollingstone.
     com/politics/politics-news/doj-suspend-constitutional-rights-
     coronavirus-970935.

84   Natasha Singer and Choe Sang-Hun, "As Coronavirus Surveillance
     Escalates, Personal Privacy Plummets," *New York Times*, April 17, 2020,
     accessed October 15, 2021, https://www.nytimes.com/2020/03/23/
     technology/coronavirus-surveillance-tracking-privacy.html.

85   Tal Axelrod, "Three States Push Criminal Penalties for Fossil Fuel
     Protests amid Coronavirus," *Hill*, March 27, 2020, accessed October
     15, 2021, https://tinyurl.com/unbpwukh.

86 "Tyson Food Managers Bet on Workers Getting Covid-19, Lawsuit Says," BBC News, November 19, 2020, accessed October 15, 2021, https://www.bbc.com/news/world-us-canada-55009228.

87 Simon Chandler, "Coronavirus Could Infect Privacy and Civil Liberties Forever," *Forbes*, March 23, 2020, accessed October 15, 2021, https://tinyurl.com/4ah7ka6z.

88 See Buyniski, "The Post-COVID-19 World," 287.

89 Ibid.," 287–88; also see Emil Protalinsky, "How Draganfly Brought a 'Pandemic Drone' to the U.S.," Machine, April 30, 2020, accessed October 15, 2021, https://venturebeat.com/2020/04/30/draganfly-pandemic-drone-united-states-pilots.

90 Buyniski, "The Post-COVID-19 World," 287–88.

91 Natasha Singer and Choe Sang-Hun, "As Coronavirus Surveillance Escalates, Personal Privacy Plummets," *New York Times*, April 17, 2020, accessed October 15, 2021, https://www.nytimes.com/2020/03/23/technology/coronavirus-surveillance-tracking-privacy.html.

92 Kenneth Good, "Escalating State Repression and COVID-19: Their Impact on the Poor in Kenya," Australian Outlook, August 10, 2020, accessed October 15, 2021, https://tinyurl.com/3m98r6ka; also see "Kenya: Police Brutality during Curfew," Human Rights Watch, April 22, 2020, accessed October 15, 2021, https://www.hrw.org/news/2020/04/22/kenya-police-brutality-during-curfew.

93 "No Vaccine for Cruelty," 51.

94 Noa Landau and Netael Bandel, "To Stop the Coronavirus, Shin Bet Can Now Track Cellphones without Court Order," *Haaretz*, March 15, 2020, accessed October 15, 2021, https://tinyurl.com/2haxnnk.

95 "Covid-19 Investment Implications Series."

96 See, inter alia, Maurizio Guerrero, "Con la Excusa de Combatir la Pandemia, Avanza la Militarización de América Latina, Alertan Los Expertos," Equal Times, November 6, 2020, accessed October 15, 2021, https://www.equaltimes.org/con-la-excusa-de-combatir-la?lang=en#.X6hnO1l7lTZ.

97 "Americas: The COVID-19 Pandemic Must Not Be a Pretext for Human Rights Violations," Amnesty International, October 15 2020, accessed October 15, 2021, https://www.amnesty.org/en/latest/news/2020/10/americas-covid19-pandemic-not-pretext-human-rights-violations.

98 See various entries at the web page of the US-based Honduras Solidarity Network, accessed October 15, 2021, http://www.hondurassolidarity.org; also see "Honduran Government Declares State of Emergency, Suspends Right to Free Expression," Committee to Protect Journalists, March 18, 2020, accessed October 15, 2021,

https://cpj.org/2020/03/honduran-government-declares-state-of-emergency-su.php.

99   "COVID-19/People in Hone Quarantine Told to Send Selfies Every Hour to Govt," *Hindu*, March 30, 2020, accessed October 15, 2021, https://tinyurl.com/4vucfy95.

100   "IIFL Wealth Hurun India Rich List 2020," September 29, 2020, accessed October 15, 2021, https://www.hurunindia.net/copy-of-iifl-wealth-hurun-ap-and-tg.

101   William I. Robinson, "The Next Economic Crisis: Digital Capitalism and Global Police State," *Race and Class*, 2018.

102   See Robinson, *The Global Police State*.

103   Stanley McChrystal and Chris Fussell, "What 9/11 Taught Us About Leadership in a Crisis," *New York Times*, March 23, 2020, accessed October 15, 2021, https://www.nytimes.com/2020/03/23/opinion/coronavirus-mcchrystal-leadership.html.

104   I have been writing on this matter for nearly three decades now; for my latest iterations, see William I. Robinson, *Into the Tempest: Essays on the New Global Capitalism* (Chicago: Haymarket, 2018); William I. Robinson, *The Global Police State*.

105   Ronald W. Cox, "The Crisis of Capitalism through Global Value Chains," *Class, Race and Corporate Power* 7, no. 1 (2019): 3.

106   The corporate research firm Rhodium provides a wealth of data and analysis on US-China ties; see "Research Topic: China," accessed October 15, 2021, https://rhg.com/research-topic/china.

107   See "Contradiction and Overdetermination," in Louis Althusser, *For Marx* (London; Verso, 2006). There is also the larger theoretical discussion on the relative autonomy of the state that I cannot take up here, but it is important to remember that official state discourse is not to be taken at face value. As I have discussed in my other works cited here, notwithstanding Trump's protectionist rhetoric, his policy has unambiguously been to open up the United States for capital investment from around the world.

108   See "Snowbalisation: The Steam Has Gone Out of Globalization," *Economist*, January 24, 2019, accessed October 15, 2021, https://www.economist.com/leaders/2019/01/24/the-steam-has-gone-out-of-globalisation. The larger story here is that state-centric approaches violate the fundamental methodological tenet of Marxism, for which the story starts with the mode of production and class relations, from which state forms derive.

Chapter 2

1   Nick Srnicek, *Platform Capitalism* (London: Polity Press, 2016); his excellent study prompted me to undertake my own research into the process.

2   A Sivanandan, "Heresies and Prophecies: Social Fallout of the Technological Revolution," *Race and Class* 37, no. 4 (1996), 11.

3   There is now a vast literature on the new technologies; see, inter alia, Klaus Schwab, *The Fourth Industrial Revolution* (Geneva: World Economic Forum, 2016).

4   The one-third figure is from Klaus Schwab, "The Fourth Industrial Revolution: What It Means and How to Respond," in *The Fourth Industrial Revolution: A Davos Reader* (Washington, DC: Council on Foreign Affairs, 2016); this is a collection of essays previously published in *Foreign Affairs*, a journal edited out of New York, between 2012 and 2015; the more than half figure is from Klaus Schwab and Thierry Malleret, *Covid-19: The Great Reset* (Geneva: Forum Publishing, 2020), 27; the 5.2 billion figure is from ibid., 165. Meanwhile, mobile phone penetration in the least developed countries category rose from five subscriptions per hundred people in 2005 to seventy-two in 2018; United Nations Conference on Trade and Development (UNCTAD), *Digital Economy Report 2019* (New York: United Nations, 2019), 13, accessed October 15, 2021, https://unctad. org/en/PublicationsLibrary/der2019_en.pdf.

5   UNCTAD, *Digital Economy Report 2019*.

6   Thomas Marois, "TiSA and the Threat to Public Banks," April 21, 2017, Transnational Institute, accessed October 15, 2021, https:// www.tni.org/en/publication/tisa-and-the-threat-to-public-banks.

7   See, e.g., Mary Adams, "What Is Intangible Capital?" Smarter Companies, May 15, 2013, accessed October 15, 2021, https://www. smarter-companies.com/profiles/blogs/what-is-intangible-capital-part-one-of-a-series.

8   See, inter alia, Deborah James, *Digital Trade Rules: A Disastrous New Constitution for the Global Economy, by and for Big Tech* (Brussels: Rosa-Luxemburg-Stiftung, 2020), accessed October 15, 2021, https://cepr. net/wp-content/uploads/2020/07/digital-trade-2020-07.pdf.

9   Manfred Steger and Paul James, "Disjunctive Globalization in the Era of the Great Unsettling," *Theory, Culture, and Society* 37, nos. 7–8 (October 2020).

10   See, most recently, William I. Robinson, *Into the Tempest: Essays on the New Global Capitalism* (Chicago: Haymarket, 2018); William I. Robinson, *The Global Police State* (London: Pluto, 2020).

11   As reported by Erik Brynjolfsson and Andrew McAfee, "New World Order: Labor, Capital, and Ideas in the Power Law Economy," in *The Fourth Industrial Revolution: A Davos Reader*, 98.

12   United Nations Conference on Trade and Development (UNCTAD), *Information Economy Report, 2017* (Geneva: UNCTAD, 2017), 17.

13   Nell Lewis, "Seven-Foot Robots Are Stacking Shelves in Tokyo Convenience Stores," CNN Business, September 15, 2020, accessed October 15, 2021, https://www.cnn.com/2020/09/14/business/robots-japan-supermarkets-spc-intl/index.html.

14   UNCTAD, *Digital Economy Report 2019*, 6.

15   Cited in Ibid., 9.

16   "Blue-Sky Thinking," *Economist*, October 24,2020, accessed October 15, 2021, https://tinyurl.com/kf2chza4.

17   "Covid-19 Investment Implications Series: The World After Covid Primer," Bank of America, May 5, 2020, accessed 8 November 2020, unavailable October 14, 2021, https://www.bofaml.com/content/dam/boamlimages/documents/articles/ID20_0467/the_world_after_covid.pdf.

18   This data is from two reports: Nicole Rashotte, "10 Top Technology Stocks by Market Cap," Investing News, February 11, 2020, accessed October 15, 2021, https://investingnews.com/daily/tech-investing/top-technology-stocks; Melissa Pistilli, "10 Top Technology Stocks by Market Cap," Investing News, November 19, 2020, accessed October 15, 2021, https://investingnews.com/daily/tech-investing/top-technology-stocks; Investing News periodically updates the information.

19   "Alphabet Market Cap 2006–2020," Marcrotrends, continuously updated graph, accessed October 15, 2021, https://www.macrotrends.net/stocks/charts/GOOGL/alphabet/market-cap.

20   UNCTAD, *Digital Economic Report 2019*, xvii; the report noted that the comparison of composition by sector of the top twenty companies in the world by market capitalization shows a dramatic shift in the global business landscape. The number of technology and consumer services companies in the top twenty surged from three in 2009 to eight in 2018. Only two companies in oil and gas and mining remained among the top twenty in 2018, compared with seven in 2009; see page 17.

21   "Private Fixed Investment in Information Processing Equipment and Software," Federal Reserve Bank of St. Louis, Economic Research, accessed October 15, 2021, https://fred.stlouisfed.org/series/A679RC1Q027SBEA; continuously updated.

22   See Ronaldo W. Cox, "The Crisis of Capitalism through Global Value Chains," *Class, Race and Corporate Power* 7, no. 1 (2019).

23   Erik Brynjolfsson and Andrew McAfee, *The Second Machine Age: Work, Progress, and Prosperity in a Time of Brilliant Technologies* (New York: W.W. Norton, 2014), 100–1. The average growth of output per worker in the United States was 2.3 percent a year between 1891 and 1972. It was just 1.4 percent a year between 1972 and 1996 and 1.3 percent between 2004 and 2012, although it recovered historical levels between 1996 and 2004, corresponding roughly to the period in which computerization became generalized in industry and services; see Marin Wolf, "Same as It Ever Was: Why the Techno-Optimists Are Wrong," in *The Fourth Industrial Revolution: A Davos Reader*, 117–18.

24   "Where Top US Banks Are Betting on Fintech" (research brief), CBinsights, August 20, 2019, updated March 4, 2021, accessed October 15, 2021, https://www.cbinsights.com/research/fintech-investments-top-us-banks.

25   Naomi Klein, "Screen New Deal: Under Cover of Mass Death, Andrew Cuomo Calls in the Billionaires to Build a High-Tech Dystopia," Intercept, May 8, 2020, accessed October 15, 2021, https://theintercept.com/2020/05/08/andrew-cuomo-eric-schmidt-coronavirus-tech-shock-doctrine.

26   Peter Phillips, *Giants: The Global Power Elite* (New York: Seven Stories Press, 2018).

27   Emil Protalinsky, "How Draganfly Brought a 'Pandemic Drone' to the U.S.," Machine, April 30, 2020, accessed October 15, 2021, https://venturebeat.com/2020/04/30/draganfly-pandemic-drone-united-states-pilots.

28   "The Dawn of Digital Medicine," *Economist*, December 2, 2020, accessed October 15, 2021, https://www.economist.com/business/2020/12/02/the-dawn-of-digital-medicine. In Britain, less than 1 percent of initial medical consultations took place via video link in 2019; this jumped to nearly 100 percent during the pandemic lockdown; see Klaus Schwab and Thierry Malleret, *Covid-19: The Great Reset* (Geneva: Forum Publishing, 2020), 179.

29   Timothy Erik Strom, "Antennas Aflame: Cybernetics, Conspiracies, and 5G," *Arena Quarterly* no. 4, December 2020, accessed October 14, 2021, https://arena.org.au/antennas-aflame-cybernetics-conspiracies-and-5g.

30   Cited in Laurie Garrett, "Biology's Brave New World: The Promise and Perils of the Synbio Revolution," in *The Fourth Industrial Revolution: A Davos Reader*, 64, 84.

31   Kees van der Pijl, "Health Emergency or Seizure of Power? The Political Economy of COVID-19," New Cold War, April 27, 2020, accessed October 14, 2021, https://www.newcoldwar.org/health-

emergency-or-seizure-of-power-the-political-economy-of-covid-19; the drug had been in developed before the pandemic as a treatment for Ebola.

32   "Cosmetic Surgery and Procedure Market Worth \$43.9 Billion by 2025," Grand View Research, July 2017, accessed October 15, 2021, https://www.grandviewresearch.com/press-release/global-cosmetic-surgery-procedure-market.

33   Jo Ling Kent and Scott Stump, "Puppy Plastic Surgery on Pets Is a Booming Business," TODAY, July 13, 2017, accessed October 15, 2021, https://www.today.com/pets/puppy-plastic-surgery-pets-booming-business-t113801.

34   Salveen Richter et al., *The Genome Revolution: Sizing the Genome Medicine Opportunity* (New York: Equity Research, Goldman Sachs, 2018), accessed October 15, 2021, https://tinyurl.com/dcpm672w.

35   Cited in UNCTAD, *Digital Economy Report 2019*, 9.

36   Kenneth Neil Cukier and Viktor Mayer-Schoenberger, "The Rise of Big Data," in *The Fourth Industrial Revolution: A Davos Reader*.

37   Shoshona Zuboff, *The Age of Surveillance Capitalism: The Fight for a Human Future at the New Frontier of Power* (New York: Public Affairs, 2019) 187–88, 194.

38   See inter alia, Michel Foucault, *Discipline and Punish* (New York: Vintage Books, 1995 [1977]); Michel Foucault, *The Birth of Biopolitics* (New York: Palgrave MacMillan, 2004); James C. Scott, *Seeing Like a State: How Certain Schemes to Improve the Human Condition Have Failed* (New Haven, CT: Yale University Press, 1999).

39   See, inter alia, Walter L. Perry et al., *Predictive Policing: The Role of Crime Forecasting in Law Enforcement Operations* (Washington, DC: Rand Corporation, 2013), accessed October 15, 2021, https://www.rand.org/content/dam/rand/pubs/research_reports/RR200/RR233/RAND_RR233.sum.pdf.

40   Kenneth Neil Cuckier and Viktor Mayer-Schoenberger, "The Rise of Big Data," in *The Fourth Industrial Revolution: A Davos Reader*, 49; the authors describe this increase in evictions as "a huge efficiency gain."

41   Alex Ferrer, Terra Graziani, and Jacob Woocher, "Nearly 1,000 Homeless People Died in LA in 2020 as 93,000 Homes Sit Vacant," Truthout, October 23, 2020, accessed October 15, 2021, https://truthout.org/articles/nearly-1000-homeless-people-died-in-la-in-2020-as-93000-homes-sit-vacant.

42   Ed Pilkington, "Digital Dystopia: How Algorithms Punish the Poor," *Guardian*, October 14,2019, accessed October 19, 2021, https://www.theguardian.com/technology/2019/oct/14/automating-poverty-algorithms-punish-poor.

43   Laurel Wamsley, "World's Largest Asset Manager Puts Climate at the Center of Its Investment Strategy," NPR, January 14, 2020, accessed October 15, 2021, https://tinyurl.com/2v57jtpn. It should be noted that Fink was referring to a major shift in capital toward alternative energy sources. While I cannot take up the discussion here, "green capitalism" is bound up with the emerging hegemonic bloc of capital, which involves a much closer relationship to tech capital than traditional energy sources.

44   Bank of America Securities, "Covid-19 Investment Implications Series."

45   See "On the March," *Economist*, October 10, 2020, 16.

46   "Queen of the Colony," *Economist*, October 10, 2020, 19.

47   UNCTAD, *Digital Economic Report 2019*, 25.

48   Ibid., 32.

49   See Robinson, *The Global Police State*.

50   Yasha Levine, *Surveillance Valley: The Secret Military History of the Internet* (New York: PublicAffairs, 2018).

51   Carten Cordell, "CIA Awards Multibillion-Dollar Cloud Contract to Multiple Vendors," *Washington Business Journal*, November 20, 2020, accessed October 15, 2021, https://tinyurl.com/j5bby6nv.

52   See Robinson, *The Global Police State*, chapter 3, "Militarized Accumulation."

53   Cited in Brynjolfsson and McAfee, *The Second Machine Age*, 175.

54   David Harvey, *The Limits to Capital* (London: Verso, 2018 [1982]).

55   Karl Marx, "Wage Labor and Capital," in Robert C. Tucker, ed., *The Marx-Engels Reader* (New York: W.W. Norton, 1978), 206.

56   Lei Ding and Julieth Saenz Molina, "'Forced Automation' by Covid-19? Early Trends from Current Population Survey Data," Federal Reserve Bank of Philadelphia, September 2020, accessed October 15, 2021, https://ideas.repec.org/p/fip/fedpcd/88713.html.

57   Daron Acemoglu and Pascual Restrepo, *Robots and Jobs: Evidence from US Labor Markets*, Working Paper 23285 (Cambridge, MA: National Bureau of Economic Research, 2017), accessed October 15, 2021, https://www.nber.org/system/files/working_papers/w23285/w23285.pdf.

58   "The Superstar Company: A Giant Problem," *Economist*, September 17, 2016, accessed October 15, 2021, https://www.economist.com/leaders/2016/09/17/a-giant-problem.

59   Brynjolfsson and McAfee, *The Second Machine Age*, 126.

60   "Hanging Together, *Economist*, May 16, 2020, 60.

61   For a summary of the report, see Kenneth Rapoza, "Some 42% of Jobs Lost in Pandemic Are Gone for Good," *Forbes*, May 15, 2020, accessed October 15, 2021, https://tinyurl.com/ymsjkmes.

62 "COVID-19 and the World of Work: Concept Note," International Labour Organization, July 2020, 2, accessed October 15, 2021, https://www.ilo.org/wcmsp5/groups/public/---dgreports/---dcomm/documents/meetingdocument/wcms_747931.pdf.

63 See, inter alia, Ding and Molina, "Forced Automation"; Alex W. Chernoff and Casey Warman, "Covid-19 and Implications for Automation," Working Paper 27249, National Bureau of Economic Research, July 2020, updated November 2020, accessed October 15, 2021, https://www.nber.org/system/files/working_papers/w27249/w27249.pdf.

64 Ding and Molina, "Forced Automation," 15.

65 See, inter alia, Jeremy Rifkin, *The Third Industrial Revolution: How Lateral Power Is Transforming Energy, The Economy, and the World* (New York: St. Martin's Griffin, 2011); even as all available evidence points to exactly the opposite, Rifkin, a business consultant for corporations and governments, insists "a more distributed and collaborative industrial revolution" is leading to "a more distributed sharing of the wealth generated," and that in this new revolution "self-interest is subsumed by shared interest," ibid., 115.

66 Martin Ford, *The Rise of the Robots* (New York: Basic Books, 2015), 198.

67 Ibid.

68 Karl Marx, *Grundrisse* (Harmondsworth: Penguin, 1973), 692–94.

69 UNCTAD, *Information Economy Report 2017*.

70 See *World Employment Report 1996–97: National Policies in a Global Context* (Geneva: International Labour Organization, 1996); *Global Employment Trend 2011* (Geneva: International Labour Organization, 2011), accessed October 17, 2021, https://www.ilo.org/wcmsp5/groups/public/@dgreports/@dcomm/@publ/documents/publication/wcms_150440.pdf; *The Challenge of Job Recovery; World Employment and Social Outlook: Trends 2019* (Geneva: International Labour Organization, 2019), accessed October 17, 2021, https://tinyurl.com/3mrccma9.

71 UNCTAD, *Digital Economy Report 2019*, 8.

72 Cited in Schwab and Malleret, *Covid-19: The Great Reset*, 157.

73 See Cox, "The Crisis of Capitalism through Global Value Chains."

74 Ford, *The Rise of the Robots*, 26.

75 One leading software company, AVEVA (https://www.aveva.com/en) supplies software and consulting on automating just about every production sequence, including mining. On the automation of California agriculture, see Geoffrey Mohan, "A New Generation of Farmworkers: Robots," *Los Angeles Times*, July 25, 2017, A1, A10. More generally on the automation of agriculture, see "How Automation Is Revolutionizing Agriculture," Innovation & Tech Today, July 15 2019,

accessed October 17, 2021, https://innotechtoday.com/automated-agriculture. On the growth of the market for agricultural robotics equipment, see "Global Agricultural Robots Market Report 2020–2025 with Covid-19 Impact Analysis," Business Wire, October 12, 2020, accessed October 17, 2021, https://tinyurl.com/3smn2jub. For "flippy" see the Miso Robotics company webpage, accessed October 17, 2021, https://misorobotics.com.

76   Brynjolfsson and McAfee, *The Second Machine Age*, 30.

77   Harry Braverman, *Labor and Monopoly Capital: The Degradation of Work in the Twentieth Century* (New York: Monthly Review Press, 1974).

78   Cited in Jeremy Rifkin, *The Third Industrial Revolution*, 112.

79   ILO, "COVID-19 and the World of Work.".

80   For the US data, see Jose Maria Barrero, Nick Bloom, and Steven J. Davis, "COVID-19 Is Also a Reallocation Shock," Working Paper No. 2020-59, Becker Friedman Institute, University of Chicago, June 25, 2020, 3, accessed October 17, 2021, https://bfi.uchicago.edu/working-paper/covid-19-is-also-a-reallocation-shock; for the world-wide data, see ILO, "COVID-19 and the World of Work," 4.

81   Kevin Lin, "Tech Worker Organizing in China: A New Model for Workers Battling a Repressive State," *New Labor Forum* 29, no. 2 (May 2020): 52–59.

82   William I. Robinson, "Global Capitalist Crisis Deadlier Than Coronavirus (Part III)," *Arena*, April 28, 2020, accessed October 17, 2021, https://arena.org.au/global-capitalist-crisis-deadlier-than-coronavirus-part-iii.

83   Olivia Solon, "Amazon Patents Wristband That Tracks Warehouse Workers' Movements," *Guardian*, January 31, 2018, accessed October 17, 2021, https://www.theguardian.com/technology/2018/jan/31/amazon-warehouse-wristband-tracking.

84   Thomas L. Friedman, "After the Pandemic: A Revolution in Education and Work Awaits," *New York Times*, October 20, 2020, accessed October 17, 2021, https://www.nytimes.com/2020/10/20/opinion/covid-education-work.html.

85   The anxiety and depression associated with these conditions of isolation and loneliness compound the mental health crisis, as does the acute distress of uncertainty, as life becomes a permanent trauma. The WTO predicted in 2017 that depression would become the second main cause of disease burden globally by 2020. In 2017, an estimated 350 million people around the world suffered from depression; see Schwab and Malleret, *Covid-19: The Great Reset*, 223.

86   Cited in Christian Fuchs, *Rereading Marx in the Age of Digital Capitalism* (London: Pluto, 2019), 43.

87 See, for example, Matthias Pierce, et al., "Mental Health before and during the Covid-19 Pandemic: A Longitudinal Probability Sample Survey of the UK Population," *Lancet*, July 21, 2020, accessed October 17, 2021, https://www.thelancet.com/journals/lanpsy/article/ PIIS2215-0366(20)30308-4/fulltext; Mark Czeisler et al., "Mental Health, Substance Use, and Suicidal Ideation during the Covid-19 Pandemic," *Center for Disease Control* (CDC), August 14, 2020, accessed October 17, 2021, https://www.cdc.gov/mmwr/volumes/69/wr/ mm6932a1.htm.

88 Bank of America Securities, "Covid-19 Investment Implications Series."

89 There has been much written on these effects of cyberspace and social media; see, e.g., Nicholas Carr, *The Shallows: What the Internet Is Doing to Our Brains* (New York: W.W. Norton, 2020 [2010]).

Chapter 3

1   Samir Amin, "It is Imperative to Reconstruct the Internationale of Workers and Peoples," IDEAs, July 3, 2018, accessed October 17, 2021, https://tinyurl.com/5bptfmu9.

2   Stuart Jeffries, "Why Marxism Is on the Rise Again," *Guardian*, July 4, 2012, accessed October 17, 2021, https://www.theguardian.com/ world/2012/jul/04/the-return-of-marxism.

3   For *Time*'s ranking, see "Who/s Biggest? The 100 Most Significant Figures in History," *Time*, August 21, 2017, accessed October 17, 2021, http://ideas.time.com/2013/12/10/whos-biggest-the-100-most-significant-figures-in-history; Jesus was ranked in first place and, curiously, Muhammad came in third, after Napoleon. In relation to the ranking of thirty-five thousand high profile scholars, see *Smithsonian*, November 6, 2013, accessed October 17, 2021, http:// www.smithsonianmag.com/smart-news/karl-marx-is-the-worlds-most-influential-scholar-180947581; Marx scored twenty-two times higher than the nearest historian and eleven times higher than the nearest economist.

4   For the 2019 Pew poll, see "Partisan Divide in Views of 'Socialism,' 'Capitalism,'" Pew Research Center, June 25, 2019, accessed October 17, 2021, https://www.pewresearch.org/pp_19-06-20_socialism_ feature. For the 2018 Gallup poll, see Kathleen Elkins, "Most Young Americans Prefer Socialism to Capitalism, New Report Finds," Make It, August 14, 2018, accessed October 17, 2021, https://www. cnbc.com/2018/08/14/fewer-than-half-of-young-americans-are-positive-about-capitalism.html. For the 2019 Gallup poll, see Mohamed Younis, "Four in 10 Americans Embrace Some Form of Socialism," Gallup, May 20, 2019, accessed October 17, 2021, https://

news.gallup.com/poll/257639/four-americans-embrace-form-socialism.aspx. The 2020 poll was conducted by the right-wing Victims of Communism Memorial Foundation; see David Fitzgerald, "Support for Socialism Jumps by Nearly 10 Percent among U.S. Youth amid Pandemic Depression," World Socialist Web Site, October 22, 2020, accessed October 17, 2021, https://www.wsws.org/en/articles/2020/10/23/soci-023.html. For the 2020 worldwide poll, see Mark John, "Capitalism Seen Doing 'More Harm Than Good' in Global Survey," Reuters, January 19, 2020, accessed October 17, 2021, https://tinyurl.com/sbxhh3u8.

5   Chris Zappone, "Wave of Strikes Ripples Across U.S. as Crisis Bites," *Age*, September 30, 2020, accessed October 17, 2021, https://www.theage.com.au/world/north-americ; Aaron Gordon, Lauren Gurley, Edward Ongweso Jr., and Jordon Pearson, "Coronavirus Is a Labor Crisis, and a General Strike May Be Next," *Vice*, April 2, 2020, accessed October 17, 2021, https://www.vice.com/en/article/z3b9ny/coronavirus-general-strike.

6   In any event, it is worth noting that the massive injection of fiat money into the economy and the unprecedented expansion of fictitious capital, as discussed in chapter one, already constitutes a break with the monetarist orthodoxy of neoliberalism.

7   I do not normally cite Wikipedia, but one entry has perhaps the most comprehensive list of major protests in the twenty-first century, with links to original or other sources; List of Protests in the 21st Century, Wikipedia, accessed October 17, 2021, https://en.wikipedia.org/wiki/List_of_protests_in_the_21st_century.

8   APF, "Five Years On, the Indignados Have Changed Spain's Politics," Local, May 14, 2016, accessed October 17, 2021, https://www.thelocal.es/20160514/five-years-on-spains-indignados-have-shaken-up-politics.

9   Gideon Rachman, "2011, the Year of Global Indignation," *Financial Times*, August 29, 2011, accessed October 17, 2021, https://www.ft.com/content/36339ee2-cf40-11e0-b6d4-00144feabdc0.

10   "Global Protest Tracker," Carnegie Endowment for International Peace, January 2020 data, accessed January 19, 2020, https://carnegieendowment.org/publications/interactive/protest-tracker; the tracker is interactive and regularly updated. Below I will compare this data with the 2020 year-end update.

11   See, inter alia, Kevin B. Anderson, "Sudan's Revolution of 2019," *New Politics* 17, no. 4 (Winter 2020), accessed October 17, 2021, https://newpol.org/issue_post/sudans-revolution-of-2019.

12   Mélanie Vecchio, "Gilets Jaunes et Lycéens: 2891 Blessés Depuis Le Début du Mouvement, " BFM TV, December 20, 2018, accessed October 17, 2021, https://tinyurl.com/y7hbnzdx.

13   For an excellent overall analysis, see Jean-Claude Paye, "The Yellow Vests in France," *Monthly Review*, June 1, 2019, accessed October 17, 2021, https://monthlyreview.org/2019/06/01/the-yellow-vests-in-france.

14   Hao Ren, ed., *China on Strike: Narratives of Workers' Resistance* (Chicago: Haymarket, 2016), 15–16.

15   Javier C. Hernández, "Workers' Activism Rises as China's Economy Slows. Xi Aims to Rein Them In," *New York Times*, February 6, 2019, accessed October 17, 2021, https://www.nytimes.com/2019/02/06/world/asia/china-workers-protests.html; also see "China Labor Bulletin," which posts workers' actions day by day, accessed October 17, 2021, https://tinyurl.com/4dehya5u.

16   See, inter alia, Anita Chan, "From Unorganized Street Protests to Organizing Unions: The Birth of a New Trade Union Movement in Hong Kong," MadeInChina, July 15, 2020, accessed October 17, 2021, https://madeinchinajournal.com/2020/07/15/from-unorganised-street-protests-to-organising-unions.

17   Kevin Lin, "Tech Worker Organizing in China: A New Model for Workers Battling a Repressive State," *New Labor Forum* 29, no. 2, (May 2020): 52–59.

18   See, inter alia, "Over 250 Million Workers Join National Strike in India," IndustriALL, November 26, 2020, accessed October 17, 2021, http://www.industriall-union.org/over-250-million-workers-join-national-strike-in-india; Maria Aurelio, "The Biggest General Strike in the World: Over 200 Million Workers and Farmers Paralyze India," *Left Voice*, November 27, 2020, accessed October 17, 2021, https://tinyurl.com/zfd9kc.

19   Heidi Shieholz and Margaret Poydock, "Continued Surge in Strike Activity Signals Worker Dissatisfaction with Wage Growth," Economic Policy Institute, February 11, 2020, accessed October 17, 2021, https://www.epi.org/publication/continued-surge-in-strike-activity.

20   *2020: Racism, Repression and Fightback in the USA* (Tucson, AZ: Alliance for Global Justice, 2020), accessed October 17, 2021, https://drive.google.com/file/d/19wATYyqsHatDqvNQSN_41vJfVoFxfFKO/view.

21   Brent D. Griffiths, "Power Up: There's Been a Dramatic Shift in Public Opinion About Police Treatment of Black Americans," *Washington Post*, June 9, 2020, accessed October 17, 2021, https://tinyurl.com/azrfncwt.

22   "Global Protest Tracker."

23   Carnegie Endowment for International Peace, "Worldwide Protests in 2020: A Year in Review," December 21, 2020, accessed October 17, 2021, https://carnegieendowment.org/2020/12/21/worldwide-protests-in-2020-year-in-review-pub-83445.

24   Vijay Prashad and Alejandro Bejarano, "'We Will Coup Whoever We Want': Elon Musk and the Overthrow of Democracy in Bolivia," Counterpunch, July 29, 2020, accessed October 17, 2021, https://tinyurl.com/dwuc93fa.

25   Debbie Carlson, "Lithium Is at the Heart of the Electronic-Vehicle Revolution—Here's How the Market for the Raw Material Works," MarketWatch, October 30, 2020, accessed October 17, 2021, https://tinyurl.com/m73fk58s.

26   See "Global Lithium Demand Expected to Double by 2021," Mining. Com (global mining industry website), October 8, 2020, accessed October 17, 2021, https://www.mining.com/global-lithium-demand-expected-to-double-by-2024. On the percentages, see "Lithium Supply in Bolivia," Lithium Today (industry website), accessed October 17, 2021, http://lithium.today/lithium-supply-by-countries/lithium-supply-bolivia.

27   For a retrospective analysis, see Boris, "France 1981-84: From Hope to the 'Austerity Turn,'" *Socialist Alternative*, September 25, 2019, accessed October 17, 2021, https://www.socialistalternative.org/2019/09/25/france-1981-84-from-hope-to-the-austerity-turn.

28   See William I. Robinson, *Global Capitalism and the Crisis of Humanity* (New York: Cambridge University Press, 2014), chapter two, "Notes on the Transnational State."

29   For the Progressive International, see "Who We Are," Progressive International, accessed October 17, 2021, https://progressive.international/about/en.

30   For Uber, see Kate Conger, Vicky Xiuzhong Xu, and Zach Wichter, "Uber Drivers' Day of Strikes Circles the Globe Before Company's I.P.O.," *New York Times*, May 8, 2019, accessed October 17, 2021, https://www.nytimes.com/2019/05/08/technology/uber-strike.html. For Amazon, see Natasha Lennard, "Amazon Workers Are Organizing a Global Struggle," Intercept, December 3, 2020, accessed October 17, 2021, https://theintercept.com/2020/12/03/amazon-workers-union-international-strike.

31   For a detailed treatment to the matter of the separation of the economic and the political under capitalism, see Ellen Meiksins Wood, *Democracy against Capitalism* (Cambridge: Cambridge University Press, 1995).

32   Antonio Gramsci, *Prison Notebooks* (New York: International Publishers, 1971), 210–76, also see 12–13, 117.

33 Ibid., 244, 268–69.

34 Of course, demands for democratization and accountability are in the interest of the working class and the oppressed. It is when citizen rights *replace* class demands that challenges from below set themselves up for co-optation.

35 See, inter alia, my critique in William I. Robinson, "Marx After Post-Narratives: A Critical Reading of Ronaldo Munck's Critical Reading of Marx," *Global Discourse* 7, no. 4 (2017), accessed October 17, 2021, http://robinson.faculty.soc.ucsb.edu/Assets/pdf/MarxAfterPostNarratives.pdf.

36 Postmodernism and the identitarian paradigm may have originated in the West and in particular in the United States, however, the scholarly agenda set by universities and think tanks in the former First World is funded and shaped by foundations tied to transnational corporate capital. Research agendas originating in the United States often become hegemonic globally, framing the university curriculum in the former Third World; see, inter alia: Michael Barker, *Under the Mask of Philanthropy* (Leicester, UK: Hextall Press, 2017); William I. Robinson, *Promoting Polyarchy: Globalization, U.S. Intervention, and Hegemony* (Cambridge: Cambridge University Press, 1996).

37 "An Interview with Political Scientist Adolph Reed, Jr. on the New York Times' 1619 Project," World Socialist Web Site, December 20, 2019, accessed October 17, 2021, https://www.wsws.org/en/articles/2019/12/20/reed-d20.html.

38 There is a large and growing body of literature critical of the identitarian paradigm, the "diversity" agenda, and the "antiracist" politics that flow from them, way to vast to list here. Among them are works by political scientists Adolph Reed, Jr. and Cedric Johnson; see, inter alia, Adolph Reed, Jr., "The Splendors and Miseries of the Anti-Racist 'Left,'" Nonsite, November 6, 2016, accessed October 17, 2021, https://nonsite.org/splendors-and-miseries-of-the-antiracist-left-2; Adolph Reed, Jr., "Antiracism: A Neoliberal Alternative to the Left," *Dialectal Anthropology* no 42 (2018), accessed October 17, 2021, https://link.springer.com/article/10.1007/s10624-017-9476-3; Cedric Johnson, "The Triumph of Black Lives Matter and Neoliberal Redemption," Nonsite, June 9, 2020, accessed October 17, 2021, https://nonsite.org/the-triumph-of-black-lives-matter-and-neoliberal-redemption; Cedric Johnson, "The Panthers Can't Save Us Now," *Catalyst* 1, no. 1 (2017); also see Touré F. Reed, *Toward Freedom: The Case Against Race Reductionism* (London: Verso, 2020); William I. Robinson, "Marx After Post-Narratives"; Walter Benn Michaels and Adolph Reed, Jr., "The Trouble with Disparity," Nonsite,

September 10, 2020, accessed October 14, 2021, https://nonsite. org/the-trouble-with-disparity; Barbara Foley, "Intersectionality: A Marxist Critique," Black Agenda Report, November 14, 2018, accessed October 17, 2021, https://www.blackagendareport.com/ intersectionality-marxist-critique.

39   Azfar Shafi and Ilyas Nagdee, *Recovering Antiracism: Reflections on Collectivity and Solidarity in Antiracist Organizing* (Amsterdam: Transnational Institute, 2020), 8, accessed October 17, 2021, https:// www.tni.org/files/publication-downloads/antiracism_online.pdf.

40   For a police shootings data base, see "Fatal Force," *Washington Post*, accessed October 17, 2021, https://www.washingtonpost.com/ graphics/investigations/police-shootings-database; the data base is regularly updated.

41   "Death on the Job: The Toll of Neglect, 2018," AFL-CIO, October 6, 2020, accessed October 17, 2021, https://aflcio.org/reports/death job-toll-neglect-2020; for the global figure, see, "Safety and Health at Work," International Labour Organization, accessed October 17, 2021, http://www.ilo.org/global/topics/safety-and-health-at-work/ lang--de/index.htm.

42   Dana Loomis and David Richardson, "Race and the Risk of Fatal Injury at Work," *American Journal of Public Health* 88, no. 1 (January 1998), accessed October 17, 2021, https://ajph.aphapublications.org/ doi/pdf/10.2105/AJPH.88.1.40.

43   See, for instance, Robert Reich, "Trump Stokes Division with Racism and Rage—and the American Oligarchy Purrs," *Guardian*, June 14, 2020, accessed October 17, 2021, https://www.theguardian.com/ commentisfree/2020/jun/14/donald-trump-racism-american-oligarchy.

44   "Black Lives Matter: The George Floyd Effect," *Economist*, December 12, 2020, 29.

45   See ibid.; Shafi and Nagdee, *Recovering Antiracism*. Cedric Johnson does not mince his words (and I concur with him): "Black Lives Matter sentiment is essentially a militant expression of racial liberalism," cited in Johnson, "The Triumph of Black Lives Matter and Neoliberal Redemption." In what was a fracturing of the BLM movement, at least ten local BLM chapters broke with the umbrella Black Lives Matter Global Network (BLMGN) in 2020 and 2021, denouncing its bureaucratic middle-class leadership. Calling themselves the BLM10, in a February 2021 statement they denounced the Global Network, which they described as "a top-down dogmatic organization that promotes certain chapters that choose to align with their direction and sequester the ones that don't.... [I]n doing this, they received substantial donations and

funding… [working] to undermine a grassroots movement by capitalizing on unpaid labor, suppressing any internal attempt at democracy, commodifying Black death, and profiting from the same pain and suffering inflicted on Black communities. The BLM name is now being used to sell products, acquire book deals, T.V. deals, and speaking engagements. We are opposed to the movement to substitute Black capitalism for white capitalism." The statement went on to denounce the close relationship between the BLMGN and the Democratic Party; see "'To Ally with the Democratic Party Is to Ally against Ourselves': BLM Inland Empire Breaks with BLM Global Network," Left Voice, February 4, 2021, accessed October 17, 2021, https://tinyurl.com/49y2menp.

46   Karl Marx and Frederick Engels, "Manifesto of the Communist Party," in *The Marx-Engels Reader*, edited by Robert C. Tucker (New York: Norton and Norton, 1978), 496.

47   Barker, *Under the Mask of Philanthropy*, 217.

48   Among other places, Gramsci developed the notions of passive revolution and *transformismo* and discussed fraud and corruption in his various writings on Italian history. There is no one section in his *Selections from Prison Notebooks* (1972), but see in particular 52–120.

49   Hilbourne A. Watson, *Errol Walton Barrow and the Postwar Transformation of Barbados: The Late Colonial Period* (Kingston, JM: University of the West Indies Press, 2020), 256.

50   Ibid., 85; Watson is referencing Susan Buck-Morss, *Hegel, Haiti and Universal History* (Pittsburgh: University of Pittsburgh Press, 2009).

51   For the Philippines, see "Philippines' Duterte Scores Record High Rating, Despite Virus Crisis," Reuters, October 5, 2020, accessed October 18, 2021, https://tinyurl.com/y8u7bt34. For India, see "PM Modi's High Approval Rating among World Leaders Matter of Pride for Indians: JP Nadda," Business Today, January 2, 2021, accessed October 18, 2021, https://tinyurl.com/358fsfp2.

52   See, inter alia, William I. Robinson, "Global Capitalist Crisis and Twenty-First Century Fascism: Beyond the Trump Hype," *Science and Society* 83, no. 2 (April 2019): 481–509, accessed October 18, 2021, http://robinson.faculty.soc.ucsb.edu/Assets/pdf/FascismbeyondTrump.pdf; William I. Robinson, *Global Capitalism and the Crisis of Humanity* (New York: Cambridge University Press, 2014), chapter five; William I. Robinson, *The Global Police State* (London: Pluto, 2020), chapter four.

53   On the rise of neofascist movements in many of these countries in turn of the century Europe, see, inter alia, Robert O. Paxon, *The Anatomy of Fascism* (New York: Vintage Books, 2004). In the second decade of the twenty-first century, and especially concurrent with

Trump's election in the United States, these new far-right and neofascist movements experienced an upsurge, often winning seats in national legislatures. These include the Freedom Party in Austria, the National Front in France, New Dawn in Greece, Alternative for Germany in Germany, both the Jobbik Party (Movement for a Better Hungary) and the Fidesz party of Prime Minister Viktor Orban in Hungary, Slovakia's People's Party–Our Slovakia, Holland's Party for Freedom, Forza Nuova in Italy (although the Northern League is far-right, it could not, I believe, be characterized as extreme right/neofascist). Very useful also is Nick Robins-Early and Willa Frej, "A Guide to the Far-Right Power Players Tearing Europe Apart," Huffington Post, August 25, 2018, accessed October 18, 2021, https://www.huffpost.com/entry/guide-far-right-players-europe_n_5b7bf18ee4b0a5b1febee47a.

54　While I cannot take up these issues here, only part of the story of the Trump electoral triumph was the racist mobilization of white workers and the petty-bourgeoisie. The flip side of this mobilization was widespread voter suppression and disenfranchisement of voters from racially oppressed communities.

55　See Anabel Sosa, "Who Are the Wolverine Watchmen, the Group Allegedly Part of Thwarted Plan to Kidnap Michigan Governor?" *Inside Edition*, October 14, 2020, accessed October 18, 2021, https://tinyurl.com/4pzz2eam.

56　Todd C. Frankel, "A Majority of People Arrested for Capitol Riot Had a History of Financial Trouble," *Washington Post*, February 10, 2021, accessed October 18, 2021, https://www.washingtonpost.com/business/2021/02/10/capitol-insurrectionists-jenna-ryan-financial-problems.

57　See V.I. Lenin, "Imperialism: The Highest Stage of Capitalism," in *Selected Works*, vol. 1 (Moscow: Progress Publishers, 1963 [1917]), 667–766, accessed October 18, 2021, https://www.marxists.org/archive/lenin/works/1916/imp-hsc; the quote is from chapter 8, "Parasitism and Decay of Capitalism," accessed October 18, 2021, https://www.marxists.org/archive/lenin/works/1916/imp-hsc/ch08.htm.

58　Ainhoa Ruiz Benedicto, Mark Akkerman, and Pere Brunet, *A Walled World: Toward a Global Apartheid* (Barcelona: Centre Delàs d'Estudis per la Pau, 2020), accessed October 18, 2021, https://tinyurl.com/stennyfu.

59　United States Army, *The Operational Environment and the Changing Character of Future Warfare*, TRADOC Pamphlet 525–92 (Fort Eustis, VA: Department of the Army, 2019), accessed October 18, 2021, https://adminpubs.tradoc.army.mil/pamphlets/TP525–92.pdf.

60   The war game is discussed in Nick Turse, "Pentagon War Game Includes Scenario for Military Response to Gen Z Rebellion," Intercept, June 5, 2020, accessed October 18, 2021, https://theintercept.com/2020/06/05/pentagon-war-game-gen-z.

Conclusion

1   See Noam Chomsky and Robert Pollin, *Climate Crisis and the Global Green New Deal: The Political Economy of Saving the Planet* (London: Verso, 2020).

2   See, inter alia, Nick Srnicek and Alex Williams, *Inventing the Future: Postcapitalism and a World without Work*, rev. ed. (London: Verso, 2016 [2015]).

3   Antonio Gramsci, *Selections from Prison Notebooks* (New York: International Publishers, 1971), 276.

SELECT BIBLIOGRAPHY

Barker, Michael. *Under the Mask of Philanthropy*. Leicester, UK: Hextall Press, 2017.

Braverman, Harry. *Labor and Monopoly Capital: The Degradation of Work in the Twentieth Century*. New York: Monthly Review Press, 1974.

Brynjolfsson, Erik, and Andrew McAfee. *The Second Machine Age: Work, Progress, and Prosperity in a Time of Brilliant Technologies*. New York: W.W. Norton, 2014.

Chomsky, Noam, and Robert Pollin. *Climate Crisis and the Global Green New Deal: The Political Economy of Saving the Planet*. London: Verso, 2020.

Cox, Ronald W. "The Crisis of Capitalism through Global Value Chains." In *Class, Race and Corporate Power* 7, no. 1 (2019).

Durand, Cedric. *Fictitious Capital: How Finance Is Appropriating Our Future*. London: Verso, 2017.

Foley, Barbara. "Intersectionality: A Marxist Critique." *Black Agenda Report*, November 14, 2018. Accessed October 17, 2021. https://www.blackagendareport.com/intersectionality-marxist-critique.

Ford, Martin. *The Rise of the Robots*. New York: Basic Books, 2015.

Foucault, Michel. *Discipline and Punish*. New York: Vintage Books, 1995 [1977].

The Fourth Industrial Revolution: A Davos Reader. Washington, DC: Council on Foreign Affairs, 2016.

Gramsci, Antonio. *Prison Notebooks*. New York: International Publishers, 1971.

Harvey, David. *The Limits to Capital*. London: Verso, 2018 [1982].

Johnson, Cedric. "The Panthers Can't Save Us Now." *Catalyst* 1, no. 1 (2017).

Levine, Yasha. *Surveillance Valley: The Secret Military History of the Internet*. New York: PublicAffairs, 2018.

McKinney, Cynthia, ed. *When China Sneezes: From the Coronavirus Lockdown to the Global Politico-Economic Implications*. Atlanta: Clarity Press, 2020.

Michaels, Walter Ben, and Adolph Reed, Jr. "The Trouble with Disparity." Nonsite, September 10, 2020. Accessed October 14, 2021. https://nonsite.org/the-trouble-with-disparity.

Phillips, Peter. *Giants: The Global Power Elite*. New York: Seven Stories Press, 2018.

Reed, Adolph, Jr. "Antiracism: A Neoliberal Alternative to the Left." *Dialectical Anthropology*, no 42, 2018.

Reed, Touré F. *Toward Freedom: The Case Against Race Reductionism*. London: Verso, 2020.

Robinson, William I. *Global Capitalism and the Crisis of Humanity*. New York: Cambridge University Press, 2014.

———. "Global Capitalist Crisis and Twenty-First Century Fascism: Beyond the Trump Hype." *Science and Society* 83, no. 2 (April 2019). Accessed October 18, 2021, http://robinson.faculty.soc.ucsb.edu/Assets/pdf/FascismbeyondTrump.pdf.

———. *The Global Police State*. London: Pluto, 2020.

———. *Into the Tempest: Essays on the New Global Capitalism*. Chicago: Haymarket, 2018.

———. "Marx After Post-Narratives: A Critical Reading of Ronaldo Munck's Critical Reading of Marx." *Global Discourse* 7, no. 4 (2017). Accessed October 18, 2021. http://robinson.faculty.soc.ucsb.edu/Assets/pdf/MarxAfterPostNarratives.pdf.

———. *A Theory of Global Capitalism*. Baltimore: Johns Hopkins University Press, 2004.

Rosenblum, Nancy L., and Russell Muirhead. *A Lot of People Are Saying: The New Conspiracism and the Assault on Democracy*. Princeton, NJ: Princeton University Press, 2020.

Schwab, Klaus. *The Fourth Industrial Revolution*. Geneva: World Economic Forum, 2016.

Schwab, Klaus, and Thierry Malleret. *Covid-19: The Great Reset*. Geneva: Forum Publishing, 2020.

Shafi, Azfar, and Ilyas Nagdee. *Recovering Antiracism: Reflections on Collectivity and Solidarity in Antiracist Organizing*. Amsterdam: Transnational Institute, 2020. Accessed October 17, 2021. https://www.tni.org/files/publication-downloads/antiracism_online.pdf.

Srnicek, Nick. *Platform Capitalism*. London: Polity Press, 2016.

Tucker, Robert C., ed. *The Marx-Engels Reader*. New York: W.W. Norton, 1978.

United Nations Conference on Trade and Development (UNCTAD). *Digital Economy Report 2019*. Geneva: UNCTAD, 2019.

Wallace, Rob. *Big Farms Make Big Flu: Dispatches on Influenza, Agribusiness, and the Nature of Science*. New York: Monthly Review Press, 2016.

Wood, Ellen Meiksins. *Democracy against Capitalism*. Cambridge: Cambridge University Press, 1995.

Zuboff, Shoshona. *The Age of Surveillance Capitalism: The Fight for a Human Future at the New Frontier of Power*. New York: Public Affairs, 2019.

INDEX

"Passim" (literally "scattered") indicates intermittent discussion of a topic over a cluster of pages.

ABOUT THE AUTHOR

William I. Robinson is Distinguished Professor of Sociology, Global and International Studies, and Latin American Studies at the University of California at Santa Barbara. Among his many award-winning books are *Latin America and Global Capitalism* (2008), *Global Capitalism and the Crisis of Humanity* (2014), *Into the Tempest* (2018), and *The Global Police State* (2020). He has written hundreds of articles, commentaries, and book chapters on politics, economics, world affairs, and globalization, some of which can be accessed at his professional web page at http://robinson.faculty.soc.ucsb.edu. His Facebook blog is at https://www.facebook.com/williamirobinsonsociologist. He lives in Los Angeles.

ABOUT PM PRESS

PM Press is an independent, radical publisher of books and media to educate, entertain, and inspire. Founded in 2007 by a small group of people with decades of publishing, media, and organizing experience, PM Press amplifies the voices of radical authors, artists, and activists.
Our aim is to deliver bold political ideas and vital stories to all walks of life and arm the dreamers to demand the impossible. We have sold millions of copies of our books, most often one at a time, face to face. We're old enough to know what we're doing and young enough to know what's at stake. Join us to create a better world.

PM Press
PO Box 23912
Oakland, CA 94623
www.pmpress.org

PM Press in Europe
europe@pmpress.org
www.pmpress.org.uk

FRIENDS OF PM PRESS

These are indisputably momentous times—the financial system is melting down globally and the Empire is stumbling. Now more than ever there is a vital need for radical ideas.

In the years since its founding—and on a mere shoestring—PM Press has risen to the formidable challenge of publishing and distributing knowledge and entertainment for the struggles ahead. With over 450 releases to date, we have published an impressive and stimulating array of literature, art, music, politics, and culture. Using every available medium, we've succeeded in connecting those hungry for ideas and information to those putting them into practice.

Friends of PM allows you to directly help impact, amplify, and revitalize the discourse and actions of radical writers, filmmakers, and artists. It provides us with a stable foundation from which we can build upon our early successes and provides a much-needed subsidy for the materials that can't necessarily pay their own way. You can help make that happen—and receive every new title automatically delivered to your door once a month—by joining as a Friend of PM Press. And, we'll throw in a free T-shirt when you sign up.

Here are your options:

- **$30 a month** Get all books and pamphlets plus 50% discount on all webstore purchases

- **$40 a month** Get all PM Press releases (including CDs and DVDs) plus 50% discount on all webstore purchases

- **$100 a month** Superstar—Everything plus PM merchandise, free downloads, and 50% discount on all webstore purchases

For those who can't afford $30 or more a month, we have **Sustainer Rates** at $15, $10 and $5. Sustainers get a free PM Press T-shirt and a 50% discount on all purchases from our website.

Your Visa or Mastercard will be billed once a month, until you tell us to stop. Or until our efforts succeed in bringing the revolution around. Or the financial meltdown of Capital makes plastic redundant. Whichever comes first.

DEPARTMENT OF ANTHROPOLOGY & SOCIAL CHANGE

Anthropology and Social Change, housed within the California Institute of Integral Studies, is a small innovative graduate department with a particular focus on activist scholarship, militant research, and social change. We offer both masters and doctoral degree programs.

Our unique approach to collaborative research methodology dissolves traditional barriers between research and political activism, between insiders and outsiders, and between researchers and protagonists. Activist research is a tool for "creating the conditions we describe." We engage in the process of co-research to explore existing alternatives and possibilities for social change.

Anthropology and Social Change
anth@ciis.edu
1453 Mission Street
94103
San Francisco, California
www.ciis.edu/academics/graduate-programs/anthropology-and-social-change

Taming the Rascal Multitude: Essays, Interviews, and Lectures 1997-2014

Noam Chomsky
with an Afterword by Michael Albert

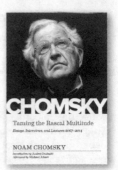

ISBN: 978-1-62963-878-2 (paperback)
978-1-62963-879-9 (hardcover)
$27.95/$59.95   448 pages

As Noam Chomsky writes about something—US foreign policy, corporate policies, an election, or a movement—he is not only quite specific in recounting the topic and its facts but also exercises blisteringly relentless logic to discern the interconnections between the evidence and broader themes involved. This may seem mundane, but virtually every time, even aside from the details of the case in question, the process, the steps, the ways of linking one thing to another illustrate what it means to be a thinking, critical subject of history and society, in any time and place.

Taming the Rascal Multitude is a judicious selection of essays and interviews from *Z Magazine* from 1997 to 2014. In each, Chomsky takes up some question of the moment. As such, in sum, the essays provide an historical overview of the history that preceded Trump and the reaction to Trump. The essays situate what followed even without having known what would follow. They explicate what preceded the current era and provide a step-by-step revelation or how-to for successfully comprehending social events and relations. They are a pleasure to read, much like the pleasure of watching a great athlete or performer, but they also edify. They educate.

Reading Chomsky is about understanding how society works, how people relate to society and social trends and patterns and why, and, beyond the specifics, how to approach events, relations, occurrences, trends, and patterns in a way that reveals their inner meanings and their outer connections and implications. It is like reading the best you can get about topic after topic, and, more, it is like watching a master-craftsmen in a discipline that ought to be all of ours understanding the world to change it.

A New World in Our Hearts

Noam Chomsky
Edited by Michael Albert

ISBN: 978-1-62963-868-3 (paperback)
       978-1-62963-869-0 (hardcover)
$16.95/$29.95   160 pages

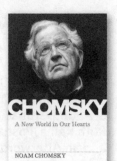

An interview with Noam Chomsky is a bit like throwing batting practice to Babe Ruth. What you lob in, he will hammer out.

These conversational interviews by Michael Albert, who has been close to Chomsky for roughly half a century and talked with him many hundreds of times, spans a wide range of topics including journalism, science, religion, the racist foundations of American society, education as indoctrination, issues of class and resistance, colonialism, imperialism, and much more. The thread through it all is that every topic—and the list above takes us just about halfway through this book—reveals how social systems work, what their impact on humanity is, and how they are treated by the elite, mainstream intellectuals, and leftists. It gets personal, theoretical, and observational. The lessons are relevant to all times, so far, and pretty much all places, and Chomsky's logical scalpel, with moral guidance, is relentless.

"Chomsky is a global phenomenon. . . . He may be the most widely read American voice on foreign policy on the planet."
—New York Times Book Review

"For anyone wanting to find out more about the world we live in . . . there is one simple answer: read Noam Chomsky."
—New Statesman

"With relentless logic, Chomsky bids us to listen closely to what our leaders tell us—and to discern what they are leaving out. . . . Agree with him or not, we lose out by not listening."
—Businessweek

"Chomsky remains the thinker who shaped a generation, a beacon of hope in the darkest of times."
—Sarah Jaffe, author of Necessary Trouble: Americans in Revolt

Mutual Aid: An Illuminated Factor of Evolution

Peter Kropotkin
Illustrated by N.O. Bonzo with an
Introduction by David Graeber
& Andrej Grubačić, Foreword by
Ruth Kinna, Postscript by GATS,
and an Afterword by Allan Antliff

ISBN: 978-1-62963-874-4
$20.00   336 pages

One hundred years after his death, Peter Kropotkin is still one of
the most inspirational figures of the anarchist movement. It is often
forgotten that Kropotkin was also a world-renowned geographer whose
seminal critique of the hypothesis of competition promoted by social
Darwinism helped revolutionize modern evolutionary theory. An admirer
of Darwin, he used his observations of life in Siberia as the basis for his
1902 collection of essays *Mutual Aid: A Factor of Evolution*. Kropotkin
demonstrated that mutually beneficial cooperation and reciprocity—in
both individuals and as a species—plays a far more important role
in the animal kingdom and human societies than does individualized
competitive struggle. Kropotkin carefully crafted his theory making the
science accessible. His account of nature rejected Rousseau's romantic
depictions and ethical socialist ideas that cooperation was motivated
by the notion of "universal love." His understanding of the dynamics of
social evolution shows us the power of cooperation—whether it is bison
defending themselves against a predator or workers unionizing against
their boss. His message is clear: solidarity is strength!

Every page of this new edition of *Mutual Aid* has been beautifully
illustrated by one of anarchism's most celebrated current artists, N.O.
Bonzo. The reader will also enjoy original artwork by GATS and insightful
commentary by David Graeber, Ruth Kinna, Andrej Grubačić, and Allan
Antliff.

"N.O. Bonzo has created a rare document, updating Kropotkin's anarchist
classic Mutual Aid, *by intertwining compelling imagery with an updated*
text. Filled with illustrious examples, their art gives the words and histories,
past and present, resonance for new generations to seed flowers of
cooperation to push through the concrete of resistance to show liberatory
possibilities for collective futures."
—scott crow, author of *Black Flags and Windmills* and *Setting Sights*

Between Thought and Expression Lies a Lifetime: Why Ideas Matter

James Kelman & Noam Chomsky

ISBN: 978-1-62963-880-5 (paperback)
      978-1-62963-886-7 (hardcover)
$19.95/$39.95   304 pages

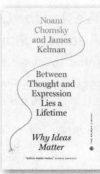

"The world is full of information. What do we do when we get the information, when we have digested the information, what do we do then? Is there a point where ye say, yes, stop, now I shall move on."

This exhilarating collection of essays, interviews, and correspondence—spanning the years 1988 through 2018, and reaching back a decade more—is about the simple concept that ideas matter. They mutate, inform, create fuel for thought, and inspire actions.

As Kelman says, the State relies on our suffocation, that we cannot hope to learn "the truth. But whether we can or not is beside the point. We must grasp the nettle, we assume control and go forward."

Between Thought and Expression Lies a Lifetime is an impassioned, elucidating, and often humorous collaboration. Philosophical and intimate, it is a call to ponder, imagine, explore, and act.

"*The real reason Kelman, despite his stature and reputation, remains something of a literary outsider is not, I suspect, so much that great, radical Modernist writers aren't supposed to come from working-class Glasgow, as that great, radical Modernist writers are supposed to be dead. Dead, and wrapped up in a Penguin Classic: that's when it's safe to regret that their work was underappreciated or misunderstood (or how little they were paid) in their lifetimes. You can write what you like about Beckett or Kafka and know they're not going to come round and tell you you're talking nonsense, or confound your expectations with a new work. Kelman is still alive, still writing great books, climbing.*"
—James Meek, *London Review of Books*

"*A true original . . . A real artist. . . . It's now very difficult to see which of his peers can seriously be ranked alongside [Kelman] without ironic eyebrows being raised.*"
—Irvine Welsh, *Guardian*

We Are the Crisis of Capital: A John Holloway Reader

John Holloway

ISBN: 978-1-62963-225-4
$22.95   320 pages

We Are the Crisis of Capital collects articles and excerpts written by radical academic, theorist, and activist John Holloway over a period of forty years.

Different times, different places, and the same anguish persists throughout our societies. This collection asks, "Is there a way out?" How do we break capital, a form of social organisation that dehumanises us and threatens to annihilate us completely? How do we create a world based on the mutual recognition of human dignity?

Holloway's work answers loudly, "By screaming NO!" By thinking from our own anger and from our own creativity. By trying to recover the "We" who are buried under the categories of capitalist thought. By opening the categories and discovering the antagonism they conceal, by discovering that behind the concepts of money, state, capital, crisis, and so on, there moves our resistance and rebellion.

An approach sometimes referred to as Open Marxism, it is an attempt to rethink Marxism as daily struggle. The articles move forward, influenced by the German state derivation debates of the seventies, by the CSE debates in Britain, and the group around the Edinburgh journal *Common Sense*, and then moving on to Mexico and the wonderful stimulus of the Zapatista uprising, and now the continuing whirl of discussion with colleagues and students in the Posgrado de Sociología of the Benemérita Universidad Autónoma de Puebla.

"Holloway's work is infectiously optimistic."
—Steven Poole, the *Guardian* (UK)

"Holloway's thesis is indeed important and worthy of notice."
—Richard J.F. Day, *Canadian Journal of Cultural Studies*

Re-enchanting the World: Feminism and the Politics of the Commons

Silvia Federici
with a Foreword by Peter Linebaugh

ISBN: 978-1-62963-569-9
$19.95   240 pages

Silvia Federici is one of the most important
contemporary theorists of capitalism and feminist movements. In
this collection of her work spanning over twenty years, she provides
a detailed history and critique of the politics of the commons from a
feminist perspective. In her clear and combative voice, Federici provides
readers with an analysis of some of the key issues and debates in
contemporary thinking on this subject.

Drawing on rich historical research, she maps the connections
between the previous forms of enclosure that occurred with the
birth of capitalism and the destruction of the commons and the "new
enclosures" at the heart of the present phase of global capitalist
accumulation. Considering the commons from a feminist perspective,
this collection centers on women and reproductive work as crucial to
both our economic survival and the construction of a world free from
the hierarchies and divisions capital has planted in the body of the world
proletariat. Federici is clear that the commons should not be understood
as happy islands in a sea of exploitative relations but rather autonomous
spaces from which to challenge the existing capitalist organization of life
and labor.

"Silvia Federici's theoretical capacity to articulate the plurality that fuels the
contemporary movement of women in struggle provides a true toolbox for
building bridges between different features and different people."
—Massimo De Angelis, professor of political economy, University of
East London

"Silvia Federici's work embodies an energy that urges us to rejuvenate
struggles against all types of exploitation and, precisely for that reason, her
work produces a common: a common sense of the dissidence that creates a
community in struggle."
—Maria Mies, coauthor of Ecofeminism

Practical Utopia: Strategies for a Desirable Society

Michael Albert
with a preface by Noam Chomsky

ISBN: 978-1-62963-381-7
$20.00   288 pages

Michael Albert's latest work, *Practical Utopia*
is a succinct and thoughtful discussion of
ambitious goals and practical principles for
creating a desirable society. It presents concepts and their connections
to current society; visions of what can be in a preferred, participatory
future; and an examination of the ends and means required for
developing a just society. Neither shying away from the complexity of
human issues, nor reeking of dogmatism, *Practical Utopia* presupposes
only concern for humanity.

Part one offers conceptual tools for understanding society and history,
for discerning the nature of the oppressions people suffer and the
potentials they harbor. Part two promotes a vision for a better way of
organizing economy, polity, kinship, culture, ecology, and international
relations. It is not a blueprint, of course, but does address the key
institutions needed if people are to be free to determine their own
circumstances. Part three investigates the means of seeking change
using a variety of tactics and programs.

"*Practical Utopia immediately struck me because it is written by a leftist
who is interested in the people winning and defeating oppression. The
book is an excellent jumping off point for debates on the framework to
look at actually existing capitalism, strategy for change, and what we need
to do about moving forward. It speaks to many of the questions faced by
grassroots activists who want to get beyond demanding change but who,
instead, want to create a dynamic movement that can bring a just world into
existence. As someone who comes out of a different part of the Left than
does Michael Albert, I was nevertheless excited by the challenges he threw
in front of the readers of this book. Many a discussion will be sparked by the
arguments of this work.*"
—Bill Fletcher Jr., author of *"They're Bankrupting Us!" And 20 Other Myths
about Unions*

"*Albert mulls over the better society that we may create after capitalism,
provoking much thought and offering a generous, hopeful vision of the
future. Albert's prescriptions for action in the present are modest and wise,
his suggestions for building the future are ambitious and humane.*"
—Milan Rai